SEMI-TRUCK
COLOR HISTORY

EXXON

EXXON COMPANY, U.S.A.

Carson, Cal.

3210
USDOT 107434

DRIVER HAS NO CASH CA 421

FREIGHTLINER

Stan Holtzman

MBI Publishing Company

Dedication

*Trucking companies are made up of people and, like people, these companies live and die. In this book,
you will see some big companies, but it is the smaller ones that I wanted to pay my respects to.
In this day of hostile takeovers and large conglomerates, it is important to remember the smaller
companies that are often forgotten and overlooked in our quest to become financially secure.
—Stan Holtzman*

First published in 1997 by MBI Publishing
Company, 380 Jackson Street, Suite 200, St. Paul,
MN 55101-3885 USA

MBI Publishing Company books are also available
at discounts in bulk quantity for industrial or
sales-promotional use. For details write to Special
Sales Manager at Motorbooks International
Wholesalers & Distributors, 380 Jackson Street,
Suite 200, St. Paul, MN 55101-3885 USA

Library of Congress Cataloging-in-Publication
Data

Holzman, Stan.
    Semi-Truck color history/Stan Holzman.
        p. cm.
    Includes index.
    ISBN 0-7603-0351-7 (pbk.: alk. paper)
    1. Tractor trailer combinations--History
    2. Tractor trailer combinations--Pictorial
works.
    I. Title
    TL230.5.T73H665   1997
    629.224--dc21   97-26444

On the front cover: High class, not First Class, is
how the U.S. Mail travels, thanks to this
Peterbuilt wide-hood, owned by Angel and Jehan
Reyes. Windows on the hood reveal a 3406 Cat
engine.

On the front piece: Moving the unusual in no
problem for this wide-hood Kenworth, owned by
Bigge Crane & Rigging Company. This outfit has
been moving the "impossible" since 1917

On the title page: 1980s Freightliner owned by
Exxon Oil Co.

On the back cover: 1952 Sterling-White owned
by Bruce and June Thomas, pulling a Wilson livestock trailer.

Designed by Todd Sauers

Printed in Hong Kong through World Print, Ltd.

Contents

Acknowledgments

There are so many people, living and dead, that are responsible for the making of this book. Critics may complain that this book has too many California trucks or too many Paccar (Kenworth and Peterbilt) products or too much of "this," and not enough of "that." Doing a book like this is kind of a no-win situation. Not all the readers are going to be satisfied all of the time. Keeping this in mind, enjoy the book.

A coast-to-coast thanks to the American Truck Historical Society and all of its members who came through with their technical aid and for their personal experiences.

A Special Thanks
To my wife Marsha, whose patience was tested but always was there.
To Ron Stallcup of Yorba Linda (California) who transferred all the data onto computer disk. "It's all good."
To David Kolman, editor of Truck Sales & Leasing magazine of Baltimore, Maryland, for being just a nice guy.

The Freight Lines
Allen Koenig/Midwest Specialized Transportation, Rochester, MN
Kent and Denny Gilman, Yorba Linda, CA

The Reefer Haulers
Bill Martin/Produce Truckers Network, Owasso, OK
Gene Olson/Pirkle Refrigerated Lines, Ft. Lauderdale, FL
Joe Cabral/L.A.-Eureka Lines, Montebello, CA
Scott Spradley, Whittier, CA
Thermo King Corp., Vernon, CA

Down in the Dumps
Ronald and Karen Christensen, Covina, CA
Larry Young, El Monte, CA
Peggy Caley/J-Cal Trucking, Lynwood, CA

The Petroleum Haulers
Dave Vanderveen/Chevron USA, Montebello, CA
Ken Seals/Calnev Pipe Line Co., Las Vegas, NV

Flatbed and Oversize Loads
Allen Koenig/Midwest Specialized Transportation, Rochester, MN
R J Taylor/Ol' Blue USA, Van Nuys, CA

The Bullhaulers
Jim Rowe/Roscoe Wagner Livestock Transportation, Jerome, ID
Richard Fuchslin/Valley Livestock Transportation, Dixon, CA

Hay and Alfalfa Hauling
Ed Bonestroo/B & G Hay Company, Ontario, CA
Dean Berg/Harvest Hay Company, Fontana, CA

The Log Haulers
Finley Hays/Log Trucker News, Chehalis, WA
Martin Grubb, Lakeside, AZ
Marvin Ward, Redding, CA

The Lumber Haulers
Finley Hays/Log Truckers News, Chehalis, WA
Marvin Ward, Redding, CA

The Bedbug Haulers
Gill Hanson/United Van Lines, Seattle, WA

Rolling Billboards
Charlie Calisto/3M Commercial Graphics Division, St. Paul, MN
Darren Keller/Lowen Color Graphics, Hutchinson, KS

Introduction
Trucking Through the Years

Look around the room you're in. Almost everything you see is there thanks to the trucking industry. Odds are good that trucks hauled the raw materials to make the components your belongings are made from — iron ore, wood, or even sand are often trucked to manufacturing plants. More trucks haul finished products to warehouses. Trucks are likely choices to haul goods from warehouses to stores. And, depending on the product, trucks quite possibly hauled the goods from the store to your home. That's a lot of trucks — and truckers — you've got to thank for your home entertainment system, your stove, refrigerator, microwave oven, your furniture, your car or truck, even your house itself. Each is there thanks, largely, to trucks.

If all that sounds surprising, then consider that trucks have been performing these duties ever since the first models were built, in the late 1800s, shortly after the first cars. While the first trucks were merely automobiles working alongside the horse and wagon to haul products, today's rigs have evolved into highly specialized transporters that have revolutionized the way the world works, the way we live.

Prior to trucking, the railroad companies were the only ones that were engaging in the movement of goods both locally and cross country. In the 1800s, the Interstate Commerce Commission (ICC) was formed by the federal government to regulate the railroad industry. By the 1920s and early 1930s, the trucking industry was already becoming a viable means of hauling products and freight both locally, as well as long-distance. Unfortunately, the trucking industry lacked vision. Not only did problems develop between the trucking freight lines and the established railroad companies, but there were infighting problems between the many trucking companies, too. Shippers were quick to take advantage of the confusion by demanding cheaper rates and special treatment from truckers. Further complicating matters was a hodge-podge of state rules and regulations.

As the situation grew more and more out of hand, the ICC finally stepped in to set safety standards, to regulate the number of hours a trucker could drive and, most importantly for the trucking industry, to establish rates and tariffs. The measures seemed severe, but they were effective at bringing order to a chaotic industry. While federal regulations were altered and amended as necessary through the years, the ICC continued to play an important role in the trucking industry until it was abolished on January 1, 1996, and its duties were transferred to the U.S. Department of Transportation (DOT).

In August of 1935, a historic piece of legislation—The Motor Carrier Act of 1935 — took additional measures to clean up the mess the trucking industry was in. Congress set new rules and standards regarding who and how a company or individual could go into the business of trucking. The Act allowed trucking companies that were in business prior to 1935 to continue to operate over their existing routes, under what Congress termed "Grandfather Authority."

One of the primary goals of the Act was to control growth within the trucking industry. To do so, new trucking firms, or existing outfits wanting to expand their routes, were required to file a "Public Convenience and Necessity" application with the ICC to justify the need for a newer trucking company when, in fact, others already in business could offer the same service. It was a challenging process, but eventually, either a "modified procedure," or an oral hearing would be scheduled and the applicant would be heard by an ICC Practitioner (a transportation attorney). An ICC Administrative Law Judge would then weigh the evidence presented by both the applicant and the existing trucking firms already operating in the area. To be granted a license, the applicant needed to convince the ICC judge that the existing carriers could not or would not offer the services the applicant proposed. The process was sufficiently daunting to thwart the efforts of many would-be

The Teamsters

As the trucking industry became more complex, its labor force became more sophisticated and more militant. The need to organize as a group was obvious. Enter the International Brotherhood of Teamsters. With roots going all the way back into the 1800s, the Teamsters were a powerful force to be reckoned with. Truckers who were members of the Teamsters enjoyed higher wages, plus many benefits, including liberal retirement and pension packages.

However, the strength and very credibility of the Teamsters, today, seems to be in question. It is no secret that the Teamsters associated with organized crime, and this unsavory affiliation with the mob, combined with corruption and greed, weakened the once-powerful Teamsters.

Prior to deregulation in 1980, the implementation of a National Master Freight Contract gave the Teamsters the strength that the union needed after World War II. The larger carriers approved this Contract, because it was a way of stabilizing the trucking industry's biggest expense — labor. Besides, the increased labor costs could be passed along to the shipper in the form of higher rates. For the rank and file members of the union, their leaders could do no wrong, regardless of what government inquiries had proven of the union's relationship to organized crime.

However, the "honeymoon" came to a screeching halt in 1980 when the trucking industry was deregulated. Deregulation brought the end to many of the nation's largest and oldest LTL carriers. Deregulation meant that anybody wanting to go into trucking could now do so with little or no "red tape." As a result, new companies were being formed, most of which were nonunion, which allowed the new companies to enjoy lower labor expenses. As a result, the old established carriers were no longer cost efficient. Some of the larger carriers simply folded while others reorganized and became nonunion carriers.

Today, most agree that the National Master Freight Contract is history. As for the Teamsters, there are only a few of the larger LTL carriers that remain union companies. And while there will always be a need for the Teamsters, their success now depends upon their ability to change with the times.

truckers from getting into the industry after the Act went into effect. If the ICC didn't have its own objections to granting a license, arguments from the existing trucking outfits were often compelling enough to cause the ICC to deny the applicant's request.

Naturally, truckers didn't easily accept ICC rulings against them. Defying the federal government and circumventing existing carriers, the banned truckers formed an "underground" trucking movement. These renegade truckers were known as "hot freight" haulers, or wildcats, and lacked legal authority to compete with the ICC-approved carriers. These hot freight haulers were a hearty bunch of individuals, and often did whatever it took to haul a load. Despite — or perhaps because they were — dodging truck scales and Ports of Entries, and running the back roads to avoid detection of their overweight or overlength loads, these hot freight haulers, many times, offered better service to their customers than the established freight lines. A hot freight hauler got paid very well for running a load of machinery coast-to-coast; it was a winning situation for the customer,

too, since the hot freight hauler could haul a bigger load in a shorter time, effectively saving the customer money.

For better or worse, everything changed in 1980 when the federal government deregulated the trucking industry. Suddenly, both the hot freight haulers and their legal counterparts — the larger common carriers — had to contend with new competition, plus a radically different rates and tariffs system. From the government's viewpoint, deregulation held two key advantages for consumers: more carrier choices and lower rates.

For the first time in 45 years, anyone wishing to go into the trucking industry had the right to legally do so without having to go before the ICC or anyone else for permission. This, naturally, resulted in a dramatic rise in carriers, which gave shipping consumers the ability choose whichever carrier offered them the best service, the most convenient service, the least expensive service, or any combination of those factors.

With more carriers than ever competing for customers' business — and without government regulations to control what they charge — rates quickly plummeted. While common business practices would have dictated that rates should be based upon a portion of the cost of operations — including depreciation of equipment, maintenance, tires, fuel, taxes, overhead costs, salaries of employees and their benefit and retirement packages — plus a fair profit, no carrier could risk losing business to its competition, so they attempted to attract customers with lower rates. As one carrier after another followed suit, rates spiraled ever lower. Today, rates are flexible — accounting for differences in distance, frequency, availability, and other factors. However, because of competitive pressures, today's rates are not necessarily compensatory. Carriers freely and readily negotiate with shippers and brokers, allowing the carriers to win more business than ever before. Shippers and freight brokers play a part in lowering rates, too, by bargaining for discounts based upon guaranteed volumes or tonnage. This was a stark contrast to the regulated days, when rates were required to meet specified levels of compensation and the freight lines were often made to justify their rates — especially if they were too low. And while a "free for all" struggle developed between carriers, as each tried to haul more and more loads more and more cheaply, the economic regulation of the past was gradually replaced with social regulation, such as workplace safety, hours of service, emissions and environmental concerns, ergonomics, and fatigue issues.

Despite all the confusion that deregulation created, it did have the desired effect the government intended it to — rates decreased, services improved, and consumer's choices expanded. The truckers, however, are engaged in a classic exercise in Darwin's Theory of Evolution: survival of the fittest. The carriers who can best meet the needs of customers — whether through cheaper, better, or expanded services — will get the most business.

Such a radical shift in how carriers conduct business caught many carriers — including some of the nation's most respected and oldest trucking companies — unprepared, and unable to remain profitable. One factor working against many of the larger, established carriers was the Teamsters Union; quite simply, the larger, existing trucking companies had unionized workforces, while the smaller, new carriers didn't. Union labor contracts frequently result in higher labor costs for employers (in exchange for many advantages over non union labor forces). Those higher labor costs were just one of many higher operating costs that larger carriers were — and are — burdened with. Companies that didn't react quickly and effectively to play by the "new rules of the game" usually found themselves forced to file for bankruptcy.

Peering into the Future

With deregulation, the rigidly structured motor carrier dynasty was now over. While there was a pricing structure in place prior to deregulation, the trucking industry was becoming stagnant. And while deregulation brought an end to many of the well-established carriers, it meant new opportunities for new and existing trucking companies. With greater competition comes the survival of the fittest. More trucking companies will have to excel in service if they are expected to survive and compete in a no-holds-barred business environment. And there will be many casualties, until only the most cost-efficient carriers survive.

Accordingly, some experts see a gradual reduction in the number of Class 8 big rigs, as the nation continues to move from a manufacturing-based economy to a service-based one. And some say that a plain vanilla or generic truck may be the truck of the future, because such a rig could be more efficient and more cost-effective.

As the playing field continues to change, there are those who believe the independent owner/operators will still play an important role in trucking. But they see major changes in the roles that they'll play and the freedoms they currently enjoy. Many see it as inevitable that an owner/operator will be more tightly controlled by the company for which he or she pulls. Some even believe that the carrier company may dictate to the owner/operators what kinds of trucks or trailer they can buy, based upon the carrier's costs.

But other leaders in the trucking industry say that the truckload (TL) phase of the industry will be moving toward company-owned equipment rather than depending on the owner/operators, because it is the only way of controlling costs.

All agree that production quantities will ultimately answer many of the questions about the future of trucking — a banner year and increasing Gross National Product (GNP) figures would bode well for the trucking industry, but anything less could be disasterous — especially for the independent truckers.

Of course, no one knows for sure what the future will bring for those in trucking, but if the past is any indication, trucks and the people who operate them will be here for a long time to come.

Trucking Milestones

1904 - First year truck registrations counted separately from those of automobiles; 7,000 trucks officially registered. Manufacturers of trucks included: Winton (since 1898); Autocar (since 1899); both Mack and White (since 1900); Rapid, which was later to become GMC (since 1902); and Reo. Truck fleets became popular methods of transporting goods for companies like Cudahy Packing, Budweiser Beer, and the U.S. Post Office. Early steering tillers replaced by the steering wheel. Most engines moved to the front section of the truck. Pneumatic tires were used on nearly all cars and light trucks, but larger rigs still used solid rubber tires. First four-wheel-drive car was introduced.

1905 - Ford, Dart, Packard and Oldsmobile were making trucks. Pennsylvania issued first license tags. Truck drivers in New York City were making $20 a week and wagon drivers were getting $14 a week. Cars and trucks could be bought on installment plans. Ford and Franklin made straight-eights for their racing cars, and Dayton wheels became available.

1906 - Marmon automobiles used aluminum extensively in production of its car. The use of the gas turbine is discussed by engineers as a power unit. New England Telephone & Telegraph has a three-ton truck complete with a power winch.

1907 - First International Harvester, Euclid, and Sternberg (later known as Sterling) hit the trucking market. A truck-trailer train having three trailers, hauls a 20-ton load at a speed of 6 miles per hour. Truckers ask manufacturers for interchangeable engines to solve maintenance problems.

1908 - General Motors is incorporated. First Model T Ford is made. Also, the first Overland (Willys) truck is made. The first concrete highways become a reality, north of Detroit, Michigan. Rhode Island issues the first state driver's license. Also in this year, Marmon develops the V-4 engine, the first self-sealing innertube is available, silent timing chains come into being, and baked enamel finishes for paint jobs are born.

1909 - At New York Truck Show, 90 percent of all engines shown are four-cycle type; 64 percent have four cylinders, while 36 percent have two, and most trucks are chain-driven. All trucks above one-ton have solid tires.

1910 - Federal makes its first truck. White makes its first gasoline model. American LaFrance makes its first fire engine. Gimbel Bros. Department Store completely motorizes its fleet of 88 trucks. Rapid (GMC) offers factory maintenance contract. Mechanical problems are traced to unskilled truck drivers.

1911 - *Commercial Car Journal* comes out with its first issue of the magazine in March. Diamond T makes its first truck. First Indy 500 race takes place. First highway center line painting takes place in Wayne County, Michigan. First electric starter, as well as lighting and horns introduced. New companies on the American scene include General Motors Truck (the combination of Rapid and Reliance), Chevrolet, U.S. Tire, Eaton Manufacturing, and Midland-Ross.

1912 - Brass caution plate reading "Overloading or overspeeding will void your warranty" appears. The federal government establishes standards for trucks in government service. First Brockway, FWD (Four Wheel Drive), and Stewart trucks are built. Armstrong Rubber and the Budd Company are organized.

1913 - The Lincoln Highway, a 3,400-mile stretch running through 13 states, is dedicated. Truck of the Year is a Jeffery "Quad," with its four-wheel drive, four-wheel steering, and four-wheel braking capacity. Ford builds 1,000 cars a day. The brewing industry is the largest user of trucks. At this time, 170 makers produced 51,586 trucks.

1914 - Fruehauf Trailers is formed, as is Dodge Bros. Mack Trucks introduces its AC Bulldog models. Cleveland, Ohio, has the first traffic lights, and Detroit has the first "stop" signs. Most truck makers do not accept the use of trailers except at slower speeds on level land. Ford establishes the $5-a-day minimum wage. Pull-More Truck Company builds a tilt-cab.

1915 - Kenworth makes its first truck. Packard builds first 12-cylinder engines and is also first with all-aluminum pistons. General Tire Company is founded.

1916 - Truck production continues at a high level despite the war in Europe creating material shortages. U.S. Army uses trucks in Mexico as part of a supply train. Self-starters are now standard on most trucks. Stoplights, windshield wipers, and mirrors are becoming popular on many trucks. First Federal Aid Road

Act becomes a reality. Goodyear demonstrates pneumatic tires on the Akron to Boston run.

1917 - War declared on Germany by the U.S. War Department, which then asks for bids on 70,000 trucks. Ford makes its first Model T truck. Dodge builds its first truck. Highway builds its first trailer.

1918 - Because of the war, truck production is boosted to 227,000 units. Chevrolet and Oshkosh build their first trucks. War hastens the recognition of trucks as long-haul carriers. Wisconsin becomes first state to make highway route number signs. Air brakes are introduced. Enclosed truck cabs become optional for most trucks made. United Motors and Chevrolet become part of the GM family.

1919 - Pneumatic tires are now offered for larger trucks. First transcontinental trip made by U.S. Army convoy. First three-colored traffic light installed in Detroit. Oregon has first gasoline tax.

1920 - Railroad strike shows the importance of trucking, both locally and in running long distances. States get surplus military trucks for highway construction. Duesenberg is the first U.S. car to have a straight-eight engine and four-wheel brakes.

1921 - U.S. Post Office has 3,850 trucks in 262 cities. Ford has over 55 percent of output for the industry. Engines and transmissions are redesigned for greater speeds over improved highways. Solid rubber tires are becoming obsolete on larger trucks. Dr. Thomas Midgely, Jr., proves the effectiveness of tetraethyl lead in gasoline.

1922 - Balloon tires and air cleaners start to appear. Gas gauges start to be seen on car instrument panels. New York Railroad starts container service. Fageol builds first "true" intercity bus on low, wide chassis. First Graham Bros. truck uses Dodge components.

1923 - Ethyl is developed by GM research lab and is offered by Standard Oil Company. First Chrysler car has high-speed engine and four-wheel brakes. First Duro lacquer paint is created.

1924 - National Transportation Conference in Washington says that trucks and railroads should cooperate and not compete against each other. Western Electric, of New York City, has the largest fleet of trucks in the nation with 12,032 trucks. First codes set up for traffic laws and ordinances. Cadillac brings out the synchro-mesh transmission.

1925 - First Interstate Highway System is established. The U.S. Supreme Court rules that states can-

not refuse to license vehicles using interstate highways within the borders. American Express Company replaces 168 of its horse-drawn vehicles with 84 electric-powered trucks. GMC trucks have four-wheel brakes as standard equipment on their vehicles. Highway signs become standardized.

1926 - The ICC investigates competition between trucks and the railroads. "Cannon Ball" Baker drives a two-ton GMC truck, fully loaded, from New York to San Francisco in just five days, 17-1/2 hours. Ford starts a five-day work week.

1927 - Most trucks now offer complete equipment, including bumpers, windshield wipers, and air cleaners. The last Model T is made on May 26th. First Divco truck is made. Mack experiments with high-speed diesel engines. Fageol Bros. produces first "integral" bus with engine under the floor.

1928 - First coast-to-coast bus service. Ford's new Model A 1-1/2 ton truck has four-wheel brakes and 40-horsepower engine. There is now one truck for every 36 persons in the United States.

1929 - White adds six-cylinder engine with seven main bearings. Chevrolet offers six-cylinder OHV (overhead valve) engine. Timken introduces tandem drive. Utility Trailer Company offers third axle for trucks. Allison joins General Motors. Leece-Neville introduces the voltage regulator. Domestic truck sales reach an all-time high of 527,057. Automotive radios become a reality, and the foot-operated headlight dimmer switch is introduced.

1930 - Truck leasing by dealers becomes popular. New Sterling engine has 185 horsepower — the largest engine in the trucking industry. International Harvester uses "removable" cylinders. Studebaker introduces free-wheeling.

1931 - First Cummins diesel becomes available for use in trucks. Relay Motors offer a six-wheeler with two eight-cylinder engines producing 275 horses. American-LaFrance beings out a V-12 engine with 245 horsepower. Zenith introduces new carburetor with vacuum-controlled accelerator pump. Ford now offering 50 different models. Southern California Freight Lines hauls 21 tons of fruit from the West Coast to New York in 117 hours running time. Marmon-Herrington is organized. Strick builds its first trailer. North Shore & Milwaukee Railroad, in Chicago, starts piggy-backing trailers.

continued on next page

1932 - The Depression takes its toll, as truck sales hit a new low as only 180,413 new trucks are built. Ford comes out with a V-8 engine. Indiana is the first make of truck that comes factory-equipped with a diesel engine. Later the same year, Indiana is taken over by the White Motor Company. White also introduces a 12-cylinder "pancake" engine. Reo makes an eight-cylinder, 110-horsepower engine.

1933 - Official formation of the ATA (American Trucking Association). Some 200 breweries will spend $42 million on automotive equipment as beer becomes legal again. Newly styled White bus has 12-cylinder engine under its floor. Sterling comes out with new cab-over, featuring a tilting cab called the "Camel Back." Truck sales are up 36 percent over the previous year.

1934 - Trucks now carry 51.6 percent of all livestock shipments. First ATA convention, as operators call for "self-regulation." Fruehauf makes new dump trailer, with power transmitted through fifth wheel.

1935 - Motor Carrier Act authorizes Federal regulation of trucking companies engaged in interstate operations. Marmon-Herrington puts all-wheel drive in Ford V-8 trucks. Cummins brings out small Model "A" diesel engine.

1936 - Fruehauf builds an integral aluminum trailer saving between 1,400 and 1,700 pounds of deadweight. Diamond T makes a diesel truck. Keeshin develops coast-to-coast network of 17 truck lines. First rayon truck tires become available.

1937 - ICC issues regulations (becoming effective by 1939) covering driver qualifications, driving rules, safety equipment and accessories, and how to report accidents. First National Truck Rodeo. Oldsmobile and Buick offer automatic transmissions for their lineups of 1938 cars.

1938 - ICC estimates that there are 39,000 for-hire carriers using 200,000 trucks. GM brings out its two-cycle diesel engine. Cab-overs are offered by both Ford and Chevrolet. Mack develops the "Thermo-dyne" engine. Two-way radio begin to be used by some fleets.

1939 - Peterbilt builds its first truck. "Sealed-beam" headlights, laminated safety-plate glass, and automatic overdrive become popular. Crosley introduces 1/4-ton pick up truck.

1940 - 160-mile Pennsylvania Turnpike is opened. There are now 3,665,956 truck drivers. Private truck operators running interstate are under the regulations of the ICC. Dodge builds 20,000 trucks for the U.S. Army. Fruehauf now offers stainless steel trailers.

1941 - Truck production goes over the million mark as the nation gets ready for war. New trucks become rationed. Willys starts making the "Jeep."

1942 - National speed limit is set at 40 miles per hour, then reduced to 35 miles per hour. Gas rationing is now nationwide. Truck weights and sizes are modified to meet the wartime emergency.

1943 - Ceiling prices on used trucks. War Production Board states need for fourfold increase in truck making if transport requirements are to be met in 1944.

1944 - Only synthetic tires are available for nonessential driving. First light civilian trucks are made since 1942. Vacuum power-booster brake is introduced by Bendix Aviation. Federal government takes over 103 strike-bound trucking companies in Midwest as an emergency measure. Wide rims show increased tire mileage.

1945 - War is at an end, as is rationing. Cummins introduces the NH-600 and NHS-600 high-speed diesel engines. Motor oils are classified into regular, premium, and heavy-duty classes.

1946 - There are now 12,774 diesel-powered trucks and an additional 5,092 diesel-powered buses. Natural rubber is used on 94 percent of all larger truck tires. Fruehauf introduces torsion-bar suspension for trailers. Bostrom comes out with hydraulic seats for driver comfort. Mack comes out with a 10-speed transmission called the Mono-Shift.

1947 - ATA launches National Safety Program. An estimated 5.5 million people are employed in truck transportation. Wire cord tires are tested for heavy-duty operations. Goodyear introduces an all-nylon ply tire. Leece-Neville develops the lightweight AC-DC alternator.

1948 - First tubeless tires come on the scene. ATA adopts trailer interchange plan. Dodge introduces "Route-Van" for local deliveries. More than 632,000 salespeople are now using passenger cars as part of their business.

1949 - White comes out with its 3,000 series cab-over model. Strick produces a roll-off roof for its van trailers. Eaton introduces electric control for two-speed axles.

1950 - War in Korea begins, as military orders start to pour into truck makers like Reo, Dodge, Ford, International, Willys, GMC, Studebaker, and Allison (transmissions). Boeing makes first gas-turbine engine for a truck. Fuller comes out with a 10-speed, single-lever transmission called the "RoadRanger." P.I.E. (Pacific Intermountain Express) develops the "dromedary" on a Peterbilt cab-over. Greyhound orders 761 diesel buses from GMC Truck & Coach.

1951 - New York enacts ton-mile tax on truckers. New Jersey opens its 118-mile Turnpike. Truck makers and the larger fleets gear up for war production.

1952 - Hydramatic transmissions are made available on 3/4 ton models of GMCs. Reo and International Harvester offer LP-gas engines as an option. Break-away brake valve is required for the first time. GM offers its first air-suspension bus. Ocean Van Lines begins container service between Seattle and Alaska.

1953 - Pennsylvania truckers launch $250 million lawsuit against the railroads. There are an estimated 76,000 diesel trucks on the road.

1954 - Nash and Hudson merge to create American Motors Corp. P.I.E. introduces air-ride trailers built by Fruehauf, Brown, and Strick. Both White and Mack introduce 96-inch conventional tractor. Ohio establishes axle-mile tax.

1955 - Common carriers use piggybacking on Pennsylvania Railroad. Tubeless tires are now available for larger trucks.

1956 - Highway Act starts plan to build 41,000 miles of interstate highways across the country. ICC bans the use of trip-leasing of less than 30 days. GM has air-suspension trailer. Chevrolet offers Allison transmission with retarder. Western reciprocity agreement is signed by nine states. P.I.E. and Kenworth develop a four-axle "dromedary" tractor, having two steering axles. Ohio Turnpike is completed. Federal weight tax on trucks over 26,000 pounds becomes effective. Last link in the Indiana Turnpike is opened, completing route from New York City to Chicago. ICC proposes "out of service" regulations.

1957 - New York Central introduces "Flexi-Van" service. Autocar introduces a dump truck with a 600 horsepower V-12 Cummins engine. Continental Trailways offers five-star luxury bus service.

1958 - St. Lawrence Seaway is opened to Great Lakes ports. Matson Lines offers "fishyback" service to Hawaii. Piggyback is now offered by 43 railroads.

1959 - GMC introduces V-6 gasoline engine, air-suspension on heavy-duty highway tractor, independent front axle and a V-6 diesel engine. Chrysler, GM, and Ford start making compact cars. Dodge offers first diesel.

1960 - ICC proposes new lighting regulations for trucks. White comes out with the PDQ delivery trucks. Ford and Chevy add light, cab-forward models. Foamed-in-place plastics show bright future in insulation for reefer trailers and bodies.

1961 - Rail piggybacking and selective rate-cutting pose serious threats to for-hire trucking. President Kennedy drops truck tax "bombshell." Private truck operators go toe-to-toe with ICC over the need for registration. The Jake Brake is introduced, reducing the number of runaway truck accidents. Ford introduces the "Econoline" van.

1963 - Fuller improved its Roadranger transmission, allowing trucks with greater horsepower to pull heavier loads. Bostrom introduces the air-ride driver's seat.

1966 - Mack unveils the Maxidyne diesel engine, requiring less shifting.

1974 - The fuel crisis comes to the United States, forcing engine builders to make more fuel-efficient engines, while truck makers start making their units more aerodynamically shaped in order to make their trucks more fuel-efficient and economical.

1975 - The start of the Federal Motor Vehicle Safety Standard 121, imposing stringent requirements for tractor-trailer braking standards.

1978 - B.F. Goodrich introduces the first air-operated disc brake for heavy-duty trucks.

1980s - Popularity of fuel-efficient trucks grows. Cab-mounted air deflectors, gap sealers are only part of the devices that are seen on tractors. Aerodynamics plays ever more important role in design of new cars and trucks. Motor Carrier Act of 1980 begins the deregulation of the trucking industry. Surface Transportation Act of 1982 allows for longer and wider vehicle combinations on the Interstate Highway System, but increases the taxes that the truckers must pay. Low profile or "low-rider" tires are introduced, as are "super single" tires. Popular users of these tires include petroleum haulers and construction (dump) trucks. On-board computers come into being and are popular with the larger carriers in monitoring and controlling their drivers.

1960s–present - From the 1960s up to the present time, the evolution of trailer lengths and truck bodies have increased as the length laws in most of the states become more liberal. Dual-axle semi-trailers of the 1950s were only 35 feet, but as time has progressed they are now as long as 55 feet long.

Chapter 1

The Freight Haulers

Backbone of Trucking

What do you picture when you think of trucking? A giant semi rolling down the highway, pulling a trailer or two loaded with freight of some sort — maybe stereos or televisions today, or clothes or furniture or who-knows-what tomorrow. Such is the job of a freight line, otherwise known as a Common Carrier. They'll haul just about anything, just about anywhere, just about anytime. And, as the most numerous trucking firms, the Common Carriers make up the backbone of the trucking industry — without them, trucking just wouldn't be the same.

Of course, Common Carriers aren't all the same. Some of the freight lines operate as regional carriers, doing business within a certain region or geographic part of the country, while others are national companies, operating coast to coast. Beyond that, two basic categories of freight carriers exist, based on the loads they haul: Less than Truck Load (LTL) or Truck Load (TL) freight.

LTL carriers usually have a dock or terminal in a city, and they typically pick up and deliver freight with either a smaller, city semi or a bobtail or straight truck. LTL freight requires more handling, as shipments are unloaded and then reloaded into larger trailers for delivery to the final destination point. LTL carriers gather many shipments together to make up one trailer load of freight, all going

"Look for the Blue-Eyed Indian," was the motto for Navajo Freight Lines, of Denver. The Navajo trucks, first dark blue with white stripes, later changed to a more contemporary shade of blue.

A Kenworth tractor, pulling for Viking Freight System, is seen here pulling a set of triples for Sparton Express, Coles Express, and Central Freight Lines.

to a major city far away, where upon the trailer is unloaded, put into a city delivery truck, and delivered to its intended receiver. Yellow Freight and United Parcel Service (UPS) are excellent examples of LTL carriers; anyone can drop off a single box of freight to ship, and Yellow or UPS will load it into a trailer along with enough other boxes to, hopefully, make a full load for a particular destination city. When the trailer arrives in the destination city, its usually unloaded and boxes are put in smaller trailers that run around town delivering the goods.

The second kind of truck line, the TL (truck load) freight haulers, is usually used only by commercial customers who need to ship large quantities of products to one of their customers — enough products to require full trailer loads. Consumers would rarely try to compare the rates of TL carriers to LTL carriers, since each serves a very different audience, but it's important to point out that TL carriers can offer lower rates, based on several key factors. First, because they only haul full trailer loads, they set their prices based on full trailer loads, thus they never have to worry about having "light" runs, that aren't profitable. Any run they make will be profitable. And even if a customer's load is "light" — less than a full trailer load — unless some sort of discount is arranged for, the trucking company will still be paid for the full trailer capacity, so that light load actually makes them more money, instead of less. Second, and just as important, is the fact that hauling TL freight usual-

ly does not require the trucker to have offices or depots in numerous locations, which keeps overhead costs low. This is what makes TL freight hauling so appealing to independent owner/operators — their only expenses are their truck, their own time, plus insurance, fuel, and maintenance costs. Third, because TL freight generally is picked up at Point A and dropped off at Point B, there's less handling involved; the freight is loaded once, and unloaded once, unlike LTL freight, which may require your package to be shuffled from one truck to the next several times, each time incurring another unload/load cycle. Less handling further contributes to lower rates.

Common Carriers can be regular route LTL companies that operate over a specific route or between specific points, but these are a dying breed, thanks in part to the deregulation of the trucking industry.

Irregular route LTL or TL carriers operate on any highway between numerous points or areas, transporting general commodities (freight), or specific items such as flammable liquids or household goods. Exempt carriers will be discussed at length in other chapters of this book.

Besides Common Carriers, there are the Contract Carriers. Most of the carriers today are Contract Carriers. Under the old ICC, Contract Carriers were heavily restricted, however, since deregulation, there are no longer such restrictions, and it is predicted that by the year 2000, as much as 80 percent of all truck shipments will be made under contract.

Private Carriers are another group that make up the trucking industry. Private Carriers move only their own products. However, deregulation now allows these kinds of carriers to hold "For Hire" Common or Contract Carrier authority to backhaul for others, which allows trucking divisions of companies the opportunity to be a profit-producing business unit.

All of the above-mentioned carriers must be registered with the Federal DOT, and are subject to all DOT safety regulations. Hauling freight or general commodities is usually performed in closed vans, in order to protect the cargo from the outside elements and bad weather conditions. Loading these van trailers high and tight is done in order to get the most revenue possible out of each load. Freight that is palletized tends to take less time, as an experienced forklift operator can generally load a 53-foot trailer in less than an hour. This, of course, depends on what kind of freight is being loaded and if it is LTL or TL freight. LTL commodities tend to take a little longer to load, because they can be irregular shapes and sizes, plus they may not be palletized.

Most of the trucking companies today, both LTL and TL operations, are nonunion in nature. While the Teamsters dominated the trucking industry from the 1930s through the 1970s, today, the union no longer seems to have the clout it once enjoyed. As times changed, as the pressures and demands on the trucking industry changed, many of the Teamster's rules were rendered unnecessary. Coupled with tough (read: "expensive") wage and benefit packages, Unions have taken their toll and have sapped the industry of its vitality.

For the owner-operator or independent trucker, deregulation has meant more opportunities in trucking, provided that they become more proficient as both business people and professional truckers. During the 1960s, favorable legislation allowed owner-operators to be treated as independent contractors, providing carriers additional flexibility and the ability to offer more services to the shipping public. There are some who say that the success of the owner-operator met its peak in the 1980s. There are many carriers, both LTL and TL, that offer many positions for owner-operators, with

Here's a typical Transcon White-Freightliner with a 40-foot trailer. The familiar blue trucks of Transcon first made their debut in 1946 and closed their doors in the 1980s.

A late-model International pulling a set of doubles for Old Dominion Freightline. Founded in 1934, this company is a popular LTL carrier.

This Kenworth cab-over, circa 1965, pulls for Garrett Freight Lines. Founded by Clarence Garrett, this LTL and TL carrier's colors were dark green accented in yellow, and was home-based in Pocatello, Idaho. In the 1980s, Garrett became part of ANR Freight Systems of Golden, Colorado.

husband and wife driving teams available in many companies.

Many of the larger fleets today utilize the services and equipment of the owner-operators, while others in the trucking industry have both owner-operators and company-owned equipment at their disposal. This is especially true in the field of household goods movers (the van lines). With a lot of the rates at 1980 levels, successful owner-operator fleets will need to find ways to pass along volume purchasing of equipment, fuel and insurance in order to reduce the costs that these truckers have to bear.

Manufacturers, too, have an important role in making better components and equipment that lasts longer, thus helping to hold operating costs at bay.

Since the early days of the automotive industry, and especially since the Interstate Highway Act of 1956, Class 8 trucks have evolved right alongside the automobile, either pioneering new technologies or quickly adopting — or even adapting — technologies to make trucking safer, more reliable, more cost effective and, of course, more productive.

The big rigs of today have little in common with their predecessors, on a technical level. Some of the many changes that have occurred within the trucking industry include the following:

· Diesel engines replaced gasoline engines.
· Tubeless tires replaced tube tires.
· Air brakes replaced vacuum brakes.
· Air ride suspension systems replaced steel springs.
· Air-cushion seats replaced innerspring seats.
· Air conditioning became commonplace.
· Two or more spot mirrors enhanced visibility.
· West Coast-type mirrors and convex safety mirrors became common.
· Safety glass became standard equipment.
· Oil bearings replaced grease seal bearings.
· Brake linings improved.
· Disc wheels replaced spoked wheels.
· Aluminum bodies replaced steel bodies.

Trailers, as well, have evolved from 14-footers up to today's 53-foot and 57-foot (in some places) beauties. Each increase in trailer length has allowed a reduction in per-unit transportation costs, which helped the trucking industry and many others in America to grow.

Usually a 53-foot trailer can haul as much as 43,000 pounds. However, this may vary and the weight of the tractor has a lot to do with what the gross weight will be. Lightweight and palletized loads are the easiest to both load and unload —

Pictured here are some of the line-haul tractors operated by T.I.M.E., home-based in Lubbock, Texas in 1927. Later this company became part of Denver-Chicago Trucking, and was to be known as TIME-DC.

power on and power off with a very minimal amount of manual labor involved. Hazardous loads, on the other hand, can present problems during both loading and unloading. Plus, hazardous commodities have to be properly secured while they are in transit, because there is a high liability connected with transporting hazardous loads.

Thanks in part to innovations like these, shippers of all kinds have been able to compete across the nation, as well as around the world, because of the economics and flexibility of the U.S. trucking industry. Compared to Russia, the United States has developed into the world's leader of commercial transportation, due to its ability to move its products by highways more efficiently and faster. Russia, on the other hand, has faltered mainly because of its inability to get its products to consumers.

Of particular concern to the trucking industry, today, are the roller coaster-like fuel prices. Carriers, shippers, and equipment makers are all working together to help reduce this major cost of operating. Carriers have been able to help cover a part of increased fuel costs through fuel surcharges that are

This 1965 picture depicts a Kenworth cab-over, circa 1962 taken in Toledo, Ohio. Colors for the Denver-Chicago rigs were green, black, and red. Starting in Denver in 1931, the D-C rigs were seen coast-to-coast, but went out business in the 1980s. Deregulation spelled the end for so many of the larger LTL and TL carriers.

added to each freight bill. Truck manufacturers have introduced increasingly fuel-efficient engines and powertrain components, as well as aerodynamically designed cabs and bodies, both of which have combined to increase a modern rig's range to 10 miles per gallon of diesel fuel — up from just 3-1/2 in recent years — thus greatly compensating for the often inexplicable fuel price hikes. Additionally, shippers and carriers are working together to avoid deadheading (running empty one way), as well as to maximize round trip movements of freight. Although the federal government has been mandating more fuel-efficient equipment, it has been — and continues to be — the makers of both trucks and trailers, together with other component makers, that are leading the way towards ever safer trucks that use less and less fuel.

While deregulation offered newcomers a chance to compete for their "piece of the action," there has been a downside to this freedom. Particularly important has been the issue of how will the LTL and

These two 1951 Kenworths, owned by Joe Cabral and leased to Watson Bros. Transportation, were photographed in August 1956. These rigs ran from Los Angeles to Denver. Watson Bros. got its start in Omaha in 1926, and became part of Yellow Freight System in the 1960s.

Who could ever forget the bright red trucks of Pacific Intermountain Express (PIE, for short). First started in 1926, PIE really started to expand when it took over the operations of West Coast Fast Freight and its sister company, System Tank Lines, in the 1950s. Pictured is a Peterbilt and set of doubles photographed in Wyoming, 1965.

TL carriers handle hours of service? Shorter or longer on-duty driving times could change the way these companies will operate. Most LTL carriers have clusters of terminals and relay stations that are built around the current hours of service. Unworkable ergonomics could stop any progress that the carriers have thus far made. Tougher emission standards, based upon "junk science" by the anti-motor vehicle forces within the U.S. government, could be devastating to the trucking industry and everyone in it. Everyone in the trucking industry, including the owner-operators, must become involved in the legislative process. Gone are the days when complacent truckers could just "let someone else do it."

Owner-operators are confronted with all of the above problems, plus the problems of buying expensive fuel, insurance, and equipment. Their costs must reflect the same costs as the larger fleets that

buy in volume if these independent truckers are to remain in business.

Busiest times of the year for the freight haulers can take place within the last six months of the year — during the annual "Christmas rush," when businesses begin stocking up for Christmas and the economy tends to be better.

It's hard to discuss hauling freight without giving at least some consideration to the problems of claims, which are usually the result of negligence on the part of those who handle or load or unload the freight. The larger carriers, both LTL and TL, have a claims office at corporate headquarters, under the control of the Claims Manager. Owner-operators, pulling for a larger carrier, can be held accountable for claims if it can be proven that the damage had occurred in transportation.

Beyond the damaged cargo claims are the worker injury claims that can often result in handling

air. The first examples of refrigerated haulers surfaced in the late 1930s, when they were used to transport freshly killed chickens. This modest attempt to keep perishables fresh would eventually revolutionize both the food processing industry and justify the importance of the refrigerated hauler.

Today's state-of-the-art reefers were born out of the days when truckers, hauling fresh and frozen items, used a system called bunkers and blowers. This consisted of an engine mounted on the outside of a 30- to 35-foot van trailer, with a fan on the inside of the van. This van trailer had insulation within its walls, in order to keep heat out and maintain a colder environment inside. Though this insulation was a bit primitive by today's standards, it nevertheless did the job of keeping things cold. The fan on the inside of the van was driven by the motor, usually found in the front or nose of the trailer. The engines were notorious for their loud operation. Inside the trailer, large blocks of ice were placed in the front of the trailer or load. The bunker was a partition inside the front of the trailer. The large blocks of ice were available at most of the truck stops, and either the trucker or truck stop attendant would place these blocks of ice either through the roof of the trailer, or from the sides. Many trailers had smaller doors on the sides of the trailer corner radius area, where the sides of the trailer met with the front part. Ice blocks weighed about 100 pounds each and special ice hooks were used to handle them. As much ice was loaded as the front of the trailer could accommodate, then air from the fan would blow across the load in order to cool the load while it was in transit. It was not unusual for the trucker to stop and cool down his load, every 200–300 miles. Besides having ice houses, the truck stops had ice crushers, and many a trucker had his cargo iced down with crushed ice, blown through a large hose that resembled fire hoses. Icing down the load was especially necessary for certain products, like a load of fresh, sweet corn.

Prior to the 1956 Interstate Highway Act, truck routes were just that — routes! Modern Interstates simply did not exist, so when a produce

Titled as a 1935 Ward, this tractor "says" Peterbilt all over it. Powered by a Cummins 262 horsepower engine and a five-speed main and three-speed auxiliary transmissions, this rig, along with two other candy-apple KWs, were owned by Danny and Gilbert Muñoz of East Los Angeles. The D&G trucks were a common sight in the 1960s, hauling produce from Nogales, Arizona, into Los Angeles.

Kansas-Arizona Motor Express had owner/operators who leased their tractors and trailers to them. Their rigs ran cross-country hauling produce and fruit. There were no standard colors or makes of equipment, as the owner/operators were free to use whatever make of truck and color they chose. Here we see a dark green LJ Mack.

trucker was running in Arizona in July, he or she had to stop quite frequently to protect the perishable cargo from the ravages of the outside heat. Needless to say, it took a longer amount of time to complete delivery and many receivers could not understand the long delays that plagued these early reefer haulers.

As more liberal length laws were starting to take effect, trailers were becoming longer. Gone were the 30-foot vans, flatbeds, and other semis. The common lengths were 38 feet and the more popular 40-foot trailers. With the increase in trailer sizes, newer demands were placed on the refrigerated unit, as both nose-mounted and under-trailer models had many styles from which to select.

The red Dunkley Distributing trucks were mostly Diamond Ts, but here we have a Peterbilt, circa 1953. Based in Salt Lake City, Dunkley mainly ran in the West.

While many styles work in much the same way, some are tailored to best preserve and protect certain types of products that may have different refrigeration requirements than other products. For example, freshly processed or cut meat requires a temperature in the high 30s to maintain freshness and prevent deterioration. Entire sides of beef can be loaded onto reefer trailers at the packing plants, on hooks and fixtures that allow them to be rolled into the trailers, suspended from the ceiling, then, thanks to the refrigeration units, they can be trucked anywhere in the country. This kind of load is referred to as "swinging meat," and hauling it can present special in-transit problems, namely because of the load's high center of gravity and centrifugal forces that act on the swaying meat, which can conspire to cause a trailer or bobtail truck to flip over on its side, if a turn is taken too fast.

Likewise, certain fruit and produce require precise temperatures, otherwise an entire load can spoil, leading to a very expensive claim. Strawberry and raspberry growers know that their product is extremely delicate, so they often insist that only truckers experienced in hauling strawberries and raspberries be used. Apples, peaches, and grapes require temps within 34 to 36 degrees, which is also good for transporting lettuce, carrots, and celery. Potatoes, ideally, should be hauled in an environment that's 45 to 50 degrees. Dairy products should be maintained just above freezing, except, of course for ice cream.

Food isn't the only type of product that requires refrigeration, however. Freshly cut flowers, various computers and their parts, photographic supplies, medical supplies and various chemicals, human blood and plasma, and even human remains must be transported in temperature-sensitive conditions to prevent decomposition.

One significant difference between hauling refrigerated loads and transporting freight is that reefer loads are perishable, so when a trucker signs the Bill of Lading, he or she is accepting responsibility for the safe and fresh arrival of the load at its destination point — whether that point is across town or across the country. Truckers should keep this in mind, because the final decision to haul or not to haul rests entirely upon them. Bills of Lading should always specify the temperatures that are to be maintained during transit. Also, a contract should accompany a Bill of Lading, and should include (in writing) how much the load pays, the pick up and delivery dates, whom to call and how often, plus any other information that pertains to the load. Drivers should also always be present to see

Walter Holm & Company was a large shipper of fruit and produce from Nogales, Arizona. Here we see an Autocar, with its trailer taking on blocks of ice to cool down its load.

Most of the Stucki Produce trucks were long-hood Kenworths, but here is proof that there was at least one Peterbilt in its fleet of dark blue rigs. For over 30 years, Clayon Stucki hauled produce from Los Angeles to Las Vegas, Nevada.

the load put into the trailer, because it's extremely important that the load be at the correct temperature from the onset by "pulping" it or checking its inside temperature. In addition, discolored packages, collapsed cartons or broken pallets should all be noted in writing, so there cannot be any surprise claims charged against the trucker who hauled the load. And produce brokers should be notified by the owner-operators at the point of shipping if there is a problem with the load. The same is true for the company driver, who should call his or her dispatcher, should there be any problems in their load. Lastly, if at all possible, damaged cartons or pallets should not be loaded, and any hot produce should never be part of a load.

Taking all of the above precautions doesn't mean that claims won't arise. Some questionable produce brokers present truckers with unfair claims, which the trucker must absorb when, in fact, the damaged product was the fault of the shipper or receiver. Unfair claims are only one problem that the reefer hauler has to contend with. Another problem is unrealistic shipping schedules, specifically deadlines that are too short.

Perhaps the greatest problem in recent times has been the use of casual help, known as "lumpers." These lumpers have been recruited off the streets in areas where there are cold storage facilities and warehouses. Lumpers have been winos, drug addicts, and drifters looking to make about $65 per truck to assist with either loading or unloading, though they are more commonly used while unloading. In the 1970s, things really got out of hand, as truckers found themselves victims of

extortion instigated by lumpers who threatened them at knife- or gun-point to use their services. All of this came to a boiling point, so in 1980, with the passing of the Motor Carrier Act, a provision was put into place whereby a trucker could not be forced into hiring or paying a lumper. If the receiver required a lumper to unload, then the receiver must pay for this lumping service and not the trucker. Some receivers took action against truckers not wanting to pay the lumpers, in the form of refusing to allow the truck to be unloaded at their facility, until the trucker hired the lumper. Some of these receivers were actually getting a kickback from the lumpers! While federal law has improved the problem of physical violence against truckers who do not want to pay lumpers, today's coercion has taken on a new form: Truckers who don't want to pay for a lumper, now face undue delays and long waits.

On a more positive note, the use of lumpers allows the truck driver time to get the needed rest and some much-needed sleep after a 2,500-mile trip. Many truckers prefer to run "solo" and not run in two-man sleeper teams. Lumpers also reduce the risk of truckers injuring themselves either at the shipping point or at the receiver's facility. Plus, loading time is often reduced when there are experienced lumpers on hand. While receivers are often concerned about workman's compensation coverage, in case a lumper gets hurt while unloading, the trucker shouldn't bear this responsibility.

Truckers hauling fresh or frozen produce, dairy products, meat, poultry, seafood, or freshly cut flowers should have some knowledge of the product that they are transporting, should any unforeseen problems arise in transit.

Normally the colors for Frozen Food Express (FFE) are metallic green with white trim . . . not so for this Freightliner. Based in Dallas, Texas, FFE is one of the largest refrigerated carriers in the United States.

Most fruits and vegetables contain water, and today's reefer units are designed to keep the inside air of the trailer moist. This means that better air circulation from above, around, and under the load will insure that all arrives in perfect condition. Also, palletized loads will promote good circulation and make for quicker loading and unloading. An important factor, related to the freshness of a given product, is pre-cooling by the shipper. Perishable loads must be pre-cooled if they are to be delivered in perfect condition. If they aren't pre-cooled, the trucker may have two options at hand. One possibility is to note (in writing) on the Bill of Lading, that there was no pre-cooling of the product prior to shipping, or the trucker's second option is to refuse to haul the load. Believe it or not, the second choice may truly be the best, especially if the trucker feels that an unfair claim might be brought at the point of receiving or unloading.

Refrigerated trailers of today reflect the more liberal length laws that have made 40-foot semi trailers obsolete. Modern semis are currently 48, 53, or 55 feet in length, since more and more highways can handle these longer tractor/trailer combinations.

As trailer technology has become more sophisticated, so has the technology in trailer refrigeration. The days of noisy bunker/blowers and loud-running reefer units have given way to quieter, four-cylinder diesel engines that provide the power to run the refrigeration systems that maintain the freshness of what is being transported.

Trailer manufacturers, working with the makers of the reefer units, have teamed up to make their trailers weigh less but be stronger to carry the heavier payloads allowed thanks to the reduced trailer weight. Newer materials — both for chassis and body construction, as well as for insulation — have been the principal factors behind the stronger and longer-lasting trailers. With much of the earth's ozone layer being destroyed by various pollutants, the world's leading industrial nations got together in the 1980s to stop production of some of these pollutants. As a result, the Montreal Protocol was developed, which features many provisions including a ban on the making and use of the refrigerant R-12, also known as Freon, in new trailers. Freon is a universal refrigerant found in most reefer trailers and automobile air-conditioning systems. Freon also was proven to produce CFCs (chlorofluorocarbons) and HCECs (hydrochlorofluorocarbons), both of which are known to deplete the fragile ozone layer that protects us from the harmful ultraviolet rays of the sun. Many of the pre-1966 reefer trailers are still using Freon, and it's becoming a "hot" item, on the part of some Third World countries, to smuggle into this country for great profit.

Realizing the importance of ridding themselves of Freon or R-12, many reefer owners are converting their existing R-12 systems to the newly approved and environmentally friendly refrigerant, R-134a. Conversions may mean the replacement of various fittings, so that there is no contamination with other refrigerants. It may be as simple as draining the older Freon and replacing it with R-134a, or it may be necessary to rebuild the entire reefer system, which could cost as much as $1,100 to complete, per refrigeration unit. Before doing a conversion, it might be a good idea for the trucker to check with the EPA to determine what other refrigerants are on their approved list.

There are several manufacturers that make state-of-the-art reefer units today; however, Thermo-King and Carrier-Transicold are the two most popular makers of transport refrigeration units. Current prices for a complete reefer unit hovers around $20,000, however a lot depends on what items and options are included. Add this price to the cost of an insulated 53-foot trailer and the total price may be about $40,000. For this reason, maintaining a reefer trailer cannot be taken lightly. Keeping a reefer unit in top condition is a lot like maintaining a car. There are certain things that have to be done in order to prevent breakdowns and dependable, trouble-free operation. Just like an automobile, the battery has to be checked, oil has to be kept at proper levels and regularly changed, belts have to be checked and replaced, and coolant levels have to be maintained.

Modern reefer trailers and systems now give the operator the choice of multitemperature refrigeration all in the same trailer. This is accomplished by having two or more evaporators operating off the same power source. At times, a trucker may be hauling produce, meat, and dairy products all in the same trailer, each of which needs a different temperature to maintain product freshness. To handle this sort of situation, moveable partitions can be quickly re-configured to create multiple compartments, affording the flexibility needed to haul three commodities that each require specific temperatures, all under one roof.

In addition to multiple-temperature systems, Thermo King has offered the Smart Reefer system, which consists of a dash-mounted gauge that displays the temperature inside the trailer, and can be used by the driver to pinpoint where or when trouble might be taking place. As a result, the trucker can take whatever action is needed, including a high speed pull-down that can drop the inside temperature of the trailer in a very short time. Troubleshooting is further simplified with 40 built-in alarm codes that tell the trucker to take corrective action before the actual problem arises.

Of course, no system is foolproof and accidents will happen. When they do, most truckers rely upon insurance policies to prevent them from go-

For its time, the J.A. Sharoff fleet was the envy of the industry. Their red and black Kenworths got the attention of many a trucker. This picture was taken in 1965 and the truck appears to be an early 1960s model KW

ing bankrupt, should they be held responsible for a damaged load. Responsible truckers will normally carry about $1,000,000 worth of cargo insurance, which will cover the cost of most loads, though some may exceed even this lofty value. Cargo insurance policies are available to cover monetary ranges from $100,000 to $500,000, depending on the value of the load.

For all the advances that have taken place, in terms of truck and trailer construction, governmental regulation, and other factors, there are still "rocks in the roadway" for the reefer hauler. But in the face of unfair claims, unrealistic delivery deadlines, coercion on the part of lumpers, dishonest produce brokers who cheat truckers out of their money, and other problems, the future can only be better.

And, despite all its problems, reefer hauling can be a very rewarding career, especially in terms of travel. Pulling a reefer coast-to-coast may find yourself in Nogales, Arizona, loading melons one day, then, the following week, you may find yourself in Georgia taking on a load of peaches. Then, it's off to Washington State to load apples for delivery to Boston or New York.

No, pulling a reefer trailer definitely may not be for everyone, but if you are happy doing this kind of trucking, then stay with it ... after all, when others are complaining of 120-degree temps in Yuma, Arizona, all you have to do is take a few quick wiffs of 30-degree air in your trailer to feel "born again."

Chapter 3

Down in the Dumps

Helping Build the Country

If it weren't for dump trucks, there would be no construction industry. They make it possible to build roads, houses, skyscrapers, and tunnels for the simple fact that they can haul unthinkable quantities of earth, pavement, or rock with the greatest of ease.

While dump trucks come in nearly every color, shape, configuration, and size — ranging from pickup truck-based units popular with landscapers to the mammoth, off-highway models that are several stories tall and seldom seen by the public in their natural habitats in massive excavation pits — they're all remarkably similar in function and execution, it's basically just the scale that differs.

Dump trucks come in three basic "flavors" — end-dumps, bottom-dumps, or transfer-dumps — and no matter which one you're talking about, no matter how heavy-duty and sophisticated their equipment may seem, they all have one basic principle in common: They rely on gravity to do their jobs. Gravity loads them up, and gravity empties them out. This is a benefit that few truckers enjoy; freight haulers and moving van lines have to count on manual labor to do much of the loading and unloading. A dump truck driver simply looks on as his (or her) truck is filled up, then, to dump their load at its destination, they flip a switch or lift a lever to tilt the bed, then smile as gravity pulls the load from the truck bed.

A 1995 Peterbilt transfer-dump seen here owned by Robert Ford. Just about everything is either chromed or polished, including the Reliance dump boxes.

A rare Hayes dump truck is seen here, taking on a load in Chilliwack, British Columbia.

Another big benefit most dump truck operators are treated to is the simple ability to have a normal home life, since dump trucks are generally used only for local work, allowing drivers to be home each night to spend time with their family. Of course there are exceptions to this rule, such as out-of-town construction jobs that may last several weeks, or the occasional trips hauling hazardous material or contaminated soil long-distances to proper disposal sites. But, by and large, dump truck driving is easier on one's family life than many other forms of trucking.

For most dump truck drivers, a run starts with getting their truck loaded. This can be accomplished by three basic methods: with a drive-up hopper, with a skip-loader, or with a conveyor belt. Each method is usually a hands-off affair for the dump truck driver.

In the case of hopper loading, the driver parks the dump truck under a hopper chute and, at a pre-determined time or location, the contents in the hopper are unloaded into the dump body (or bodies, for bigger loads) in a matter of seconds. Then the driver simply drives away.

Another popular way to load a dump truck — one that many of us are familiar with — is by using a giant skip-loader, often either a 980 or 992 Caterpillar. The skip-loader scoops up a load of material, such as dirt, raises it in the air, positions it over the waiting truck or trailer, then the loader operator turns the bucket or scoop upside down and the material simply falls into the truck.

For conveyor belt loading, a truck (or trailer) parks in a designated spot beneath the end of a conveyor belt. As the belt moves along, it carries the material up, to the end of the belt, where the material — rocks, dirt, or whatever — simply falls into the truck. Conveyor loading is not as common as either hopper or skip-loader loading, but it is effective in sand and gravel plants.

Despite the monstrously heavyduty construction of typical dump trucks, improper loading, such as by an inexperienced or careless loader operator, is brutally destructive. People have lost more than their tempers over careless loading — many, including yours truly, have been critically injured in loading accidents. Loader-operators that work for larger companies inside batch-plants are often more careful and seldom cause damage to the

An LT Mack is seen here near Oatman, Arizona. This set of bottom-dumps is owned by Carlos Fernandez.

trucks they load. However, should an incident happen that damages a dump truck inside the premises of a larger batch-plant, the company will generally reimburse the truck owner for any repairs that were needed as a result of any careless loading.

The next phase of a run involves a trip over scales, to check the load's weight. Scales are generally located within the plant, and they're used to determine whether too much material has been loaded. If so, the trucker will return and "trim" off some of the load in order to get "legal" (weight-wise) before entering the public highways. Fines for overweight loads can be very expensive, and the gross weight must be evenly distributed over each axle. Aside from getting expensive overweight tickets issued by both the Highway Patrol and local law enforcement, overloading a dump truck is hard on the equipment — engines, transmissions, rearends, tires, and brakes have to work harder to maintain acceptable speeds in highway traffic and that compromises safety.

After driving the load to its destination, a run concludes with the unloading. Generally speaking, there is no physical labor involved with dumping the load. Switches within the truck's cab, as well as switches mounted on the outside of the truck or trailer control the dumping, allowing a load to literally be unloaded with the "flip of a switch." In some cases, a "ground worker" will walk beside the truck, releasing a portion of the load at a time, as the truck moves slowly ahead, instead of releasing the load all at once. When necessary, the driver can dump a load alone thanks to the switches inside the truck's cab that raise (and later lower) the dump bed or open

and close the gates on bottom-dump trailers. With the bed raised, or the gates open, unloading happens in a hurry — a matter of seconds.

Though loading and unloading a dump truck may sound like a breeze, driving one isn't — but not because of the reasons most people assume. One of the biggest challenges dump truck drivers face is actually just contending with the heavy traffic found on most freeways and major highways.

Unfortunately, as much as dump truck drivers — or drivers of any large truck, for that matter — may dislike having to deal with commuter traffic, commuters dislike dealing with truckers even more. In fact, some of the so-called consumer watchdog groups have called for the elimination of large trucks during the morning commute or rush-hour times. And more and more commuters have been backing their foolhardy proposals. Ironically, few people have considered that if it weren't for the larger trucks, particularly the Class 8 end-dumps, bottom-dumps, and the transfer-dumps, highways would not exist at all! And while traffic congestion has increased, it hasn't been a result of truckers trying to pilot bottom-dumps through bumper-to-bumper morning traffic. In fact, rush-hour traffic congestion can dramatically reduce the number of round trips a dump truck operator can make, so many truckers would just as soon skip driving during rush hour. This is an important factor to consider, especially if a trucker is getting paid on a per-load basis, rather per hour.

Potential transporting restrictions aren't the only forms of legislation that dump truck operators have been impacted by, however. Like others in

An "A" Model GMC, circa 1948, is pictured here as a transfer-dump, building the Pomona Freeway through East Los Angeles in 1966. Holcomb Trucking is the owner of this silver rig.

trucking, the 1980s deregulation has been devastating for many long-established dump truck operations, because of dwindling profits. For those that are new to the profession and operate wisely, there are many new opportunities to succeed. And the older, well-established materials brokers exiting the business are being replaced by people who are both new to trucking and new to America.

Many of dump trucking's new "players" are from Third World countries, including many in Central America, the Middle East, and Asia. These immigrants are eager to live the "American Dream," and they're willing to work for less money, which deeply impacts the old-time truckers who had enjoyed better times in trucking. Not surprisingly, most veteran dump truckers are not optimistic about the future of the industry. Many have been forced to ask themselves, "Just how little money can I survive on?" Sadly, many will still make 10 to 20 percent less than that!

As in all fields of trucking, a few prerequisites are necessary. First and foremost, a person wanting to enter the profession of dump trucking, must know how to operate a big rig. While there are those who profess knowing how to operate a dump truck, special skills combined with common sense, are absolute musts in this occupation.

Another thing a potential dump truck operator needs to keep in mind is that, while most dump truckers are home every night with their families, their day may start as early as 4:00 a.m. and can last until 4:00 p.m. or later. And though dump truckers don't generally work on weekends, there isn't always "free time" to be spent with the family, either.

More often than not, dump truck operators will have to spend their weekend making repairs on equipment, welding cracks, replacing bearings and filters, repairing drive-train components, and so forth. Repairs are top priorities, if the truck is to be ready to roll again when Monday morning comes around, ready for the challenges that lie ahead for the rest of the week. Time spent with the family and home improvements all take a "back seat" if a steady income is expected. Needless to say, dump truck operators need to be mechanically inclined, as well, since hiring outside labor to make repairs can be very costly.

Still, dump truck driving does leave plenty of opportunities to spend time with the family. Unlike a lot of truckers who get caught in snow storms or floods, dump truckers usually don't work in bad weather, especially rain, because the materials they typically haul — sand, gravel, dirt, decomposed granite, asphalt — may turn to mud or become unusable. Plus, loading and unloading may not be safe when roads and off-highway sites become unstable and unsafe. Again, common sense should dictate when it's safe to work and when it isn't. It's also important to remember that while it may seem like a good idea to not run a big rig in rainy weather, there is a downside to letting a truck sit idle: When the truck isn't running, it's not generating any income. And since most dump truck owner/operators have no unemployment insurance, nor any disability insurance (unless they purchase extremely expensive private insurance policies), a few days of rain or foul weather can be financially disasterous for a dump trucker's family. Not surprisingly, most dump truckers are busier in the summer months, and have to put away what money they can to live off during the slower winter time.

When the weather is clear and there's work to be done, dump trucking work usually pays either a flat rate or by the load. For example, on a flat-rate job, a contractor will determine that it may take a certain amount of time to make a round trip (from a batch-plant to a construction site), and that is what the trucker will be paid for. While flat-rate runs do have their advantages, there are a few pitfalls, too, namely that the contractor might have over-estimated how many runs can be made in a given time. Such an error could result from something as simple as how he gauged the trip length; the contractor may have measured the distance and trip length while driving a new Dodge Ram pick-up truck at a time when there was no traffic, no accidents, and no malfunctioning signal lights. Any

one of these factors is more than enough to dramatically change how much time it actually takes for a dump truck to make the same trip. Unfortunately, few contractors fully appreciate the difficulties dump truck operators encounter on a typical day, looking out at the real world through a little windshield, across the long hood of some early-1970s Peterbilt. If the contractors could take the time to ride with a dump truck operator through normal traffic along the best route, they would get a much more realistic estimate of how long a round trip will take.

But getting paid by the load has its share of problems, too. In the old days, before the industry's deregulation, truckers were paid higher rates for hauling sand or gravel long distances or along complex routes (such as during spring months when many northern roads are closed to heavy equipment, like dump trucks). Today, the rates for such runs may pay more than for a typical load, but they're rarely near the levels paid when the govern-

ment regulated them.

Hauling asphalt brings in the unusual circumstance when dump truckers may be paid by the hour, because it often takes longer to load and unload, and the drivers may spend a great deal of time standing around, waiting for an asphalt crew to unload his truck — waiting in line behind other truckers who are each waiting for their turns to unload. Such work isn't always paid by the hour, however. Asphalt hauling jobs may also pay by the ton-mile or by zone-rates.

Each type of dump truck — bottom-dumps, end-dumps, or transfer dumps — presents its own unique challenges for its operator.

Bottom-dumps, which usually consist of a tractor pulling two (or sometimes three) trailers are quite different than either end-dumps or transfer-dumps. Like end- and transfer-dump models, bottom-dump trailers can still be loaded by hopper, skip-loaders, or conveyors. A hopper can load a set of bottom-dumps in only a few seconds. Quite fre-

37

A Canadian Kenworth set up as a transfer-dump. Notice the number of axles on the pull-trailer. Greater weights can be hauled with more axles because the weight is distributed more widely.

quently, a 980 Cat can load 1 to 1-1/2 buckets or scoops of material per trailer in less than a minute, while a 992 Cat can load one bucket per trailer in a similar amount of time. Except for some longer bottom-dump trailers that are typically found in Nevada, most bottom-dump trailers will each carry 12-1/2 tons of material. Incidentally, cost for a new set of bottom-dump trailers can run anywhere from $30,000 on up, depending on what make and options are ordered.

Because bottom-dumps are a tractor with at least two trailers (known as doubles), it takes a lot of skill to pilot one of these units through congested freeway traffic. And maneuvering a set of doubles at a construction site can present even greater challenges. For instance, unloading has to be well thought out, because, while it is possible to back-up a set of doubles, it's never recommended. And remembering even modest common sense will tell you that an 80,000-pound bottom-dump load can't be stopped on a dime.

End-dumps, on the other hand, generally consist of a three-axle tractor pulling a single two-axle semi end-dump trailer. End-dump trailers are usually shorter than the semi trailers that are used to haul livestock, produce, freight, or furniture, since the cargo for end-dumps is generally much more concentrated and heavier. End-dumps are frequently used to transport large items, such as boulders

and demolition debris, but they can just as easily haul sand or gravel.

Unloading an end-dump is accomplished thanks to a "wet kit" mounted on the back of the tractor. The wet kit is a power takeoff device connected to the tractor's transmission that, when engaged, circulates hydraulic fluid into and out of giant pistons (sort of like shock-absorbers) on the trailer, which raise and lower the bed, respectively. The fact that the end-dump trailer's bed raises quite high into the air presents an interesting — but dangerous — hazard to its operator. As the bed rises to dump its load, the trailer's center of gravity rises, which can make the truck top-heavy and unstable enough to tip over if it isn't sitting on solid, level ground or the load wasn't properly balanced. More than one end-dump operator has faced the unpleasant site of their trailer — and truck! — lying on its side, heavily damaged.

So, end-dump truck operators have to do a little planning before dumping the contents of their truck. The first thing to do is to determine whether there is enough room for the tractor to move forward, while dumping, to ensure that all of the material in the trailer can spill out the back. Often, construction sites are mazes of unfinished sections, other heavy equipment, supplies and people, each of which must be taken into account while planning how the unloading can be best performed.

The third type of dump truck is the transfer-dump, which is generally considered by other truckers to be "The Elite" rig. Transfer-dumpers are usually a triple-axle dump truck towing a twin axle trailer chassis with a dumping body. Transfer dumps are quite popular in western states. In some states, such as Nevada, a transfer-dump can pull two trailers behind the dump truck. Special skills are needed to operate a transfer-dump, so many truckers simply prefer to operate bottom-dumps or end-dumps. In doing so, however, they give up the premium rate that transfer-dumps can command — as much as 60 cents per ton more than bottom-dump operators, in some cases.

Loading a transfer-dump is performed in the same fashion as loading either a bottom- or end-dump truck trailer. The beauty — and curse — of the transfer-dump is its unloading process. Like an end-dump truck or trailer, transfer-dump beds tilt to allow their contents to slide out, courtesy of gravity. The difference is that the trailer is actually a two-part structure: a separate body secured to a chassis. When the truck arrives at a construction site, it must first unload the truck's bed, not the trailer. In order to do this, the trailer must be parked temporarily. If the site is located in a highly congested area, or in an area that has strict ordinances about such heavy equipment being parked on streets, the trailer may need to be left many blocks or even miles away from the site, which obviously wastes a lot of time, while the driver runs back and forth between the construction site and his trailer's parking spot.

With the trailer detached, the truck operator can return to the construction site, and, like an end-dump, raise the bed of his truck and deposit the load wherever it's needed. Then he returns to the trailer and backs up to the trailer almost as though he was going to reconnect it to the truck, but he leaves the trailer tongue low to or even resting on the ground. With the truck backed close to the trailer body, the driver can then activate a switch on the trailer that engages an electric motor to slide the trailer body off its chassis and into the truck's bed. After locking the trailer body to the truck bed (to prevent it from accidentally sliding out during transit or unloading), the driver then pilots his truck back to the construction site, then dumps the load inside the trailer body just as he did without the trailer body lining the truck's bed. Once the second dump "box" is unloaded, the driver returns to the trailer chassis, carefully backs up to it, slightly raises the truck bed, then lets gravity help him transfer the trailer body back to its chas-

A set of transfer-dumps, Nevada-style. This Peterbilt is owned by Granite Construction working at a construction site near Sparks, Nevada.

sis, and he locks it in place. That done, the operator can hitch the trailer to the truck and head back for another load.

The whole process of dumping the trucks contents, transferring the trailer body, then dumping it's contents can take anywhere from 15 minutes to 30 minutes or more, depending on where the site is, how far away the trailer must be parked, and what problems, if any, are encountered while the truck is in transit. The actual bed transfer takes only a few minutes, but does require considerable space with a solid, level surface — three commodities that can be hard to come by on many construction sites.

Of course, these impracticalities are often outweighed by the transfer-dump's number one advantage: it can transport nearly twice as much material per load as a standard truck. This can be especially beneficial to construction projects located great distances from batch plants.

Naturally, there are other configurations in dump trucking, but space constraints prevent us from getting into each and every design. However, the three types of dump trucks discussed here represent what are considered to be the more popular combinations used in the industry today, and most other trucks are merely variations of them.

No matter what style dump truck an operator may command, all agree that they're unlike any other type of truck. After all, what other rig can be loaded with several tons of cargo in seconds, and emptied just as quickly, all with the mere flip of a switch?

Chapter 4

Petroleum Hauling

Keeping America Moving

Truckers know that hauling bulk liquids is a challenge like no other. Whether moving thousands of gallons of water, milk, acids, chemicals, oil, or gasoline, it takes a different kind of savvy to truck this kind of cargo down the highways.

Unlike properly loaded solid cargo — sand, furniture, television sets, or whatever — liquid cargo freely sloshes and moves around within the truck's tank. This becomes immediately apparent when a driver tries to stop or turn too quickly, because centrifugal force attempts to keep the fluid moving, which can cause the truck to continue moving! For this very reason, hauling liquids can be a tricky task, at best.

No one knows this better than petroleum products haulers. Whether their cargo is gasoline, jet fuel, diesel fuel, or home heating oil, safety must always come first! They have to be safe when loading the product, safe while hauling it — especially if it's a flammable liquid, practice defensive driving, unload the product safely at its point of delivery, and, all the while, carefully guard the environment from any spills or damage. Truckers hauling petroleum products, perhaps more so than any other truck drivers, must closely adhere to the laws governing the operation of their equipment, whether the laws are enforced or not. Failure to do so could have catastrophic results.

Ken Bettridge Oil Company of Cedar City, Utah, runs this Kenworth tanker in Utah, Nevada, Arizona, and California hauling gasoline and diesel fuel.

Shutting down an entire fleet to take pictures, is a monumental task, yet that's what Chevron USA managed to do. The 14 Peterbilts and one Freightliner are seen here at the Montebello, California, terminal, ready to deliver gas to many of the Chevron stations in Los Angeles.

Because of the risks involved in hauling petroleum products, drivers need more than just their Commercial Drivers License (CDL). They also need proof that they were trained on tank trucks, and that they successfully completed training and testing on the handling of hazardous materials (HazMats). Meeting these rigid requirements is essential to ensure that they know precisely what to do — and how to do it — if and when an emergency situation arises.

Fortunately for petroleum products haulers, great strides have been made in tank body design and safety in recent years. The U.S. Department of Transportation (DOT) sets the specifications that all tank builders must comply with. Most of the tanks built today are made of aluminum, because, in the event of an accident or roll-over, it is less likely to create a spark than is steel.

Because abrupt motion — especially side-to-side — can cause the load to shift within the tank, the rig can become unstable and possibly overturn, easily leading to a fiery inferno if the load was a flammable product, such as gasoline.

To help prevent such accidents, tank bodies are equipped with baffles and bulkheads to minimize the surge effects of the liquids during cornering, braking, and accelerating. The baffles, which are essentially large plates spanning from side to side

within the tank, have holes in them to allow the fluids to flow within the tank, but at a greatly reduced speed, thus greatly reducing surge forces.

Domed covers on top of the tank, have impact-resistant locking mechanisms to keep the lids in place during even the strongest of accident forces. These covers have pressure relief valves that vent fuel vapors, but seals stop any liquid leakage if the tank should roll over.

Drain valves are found on the underside of the tank, in several locations, and can be shut off easily and quickly if necessary. In addition to the drain valves, there are cargo discharge lines, each with at least one manual shutoff valve. Every precaution is

taken to ensure that transporting petroleum products is as safe as possible not only for the truck's driver, but for other motorists and pedestrians and even the environment.

Loading times vary based on the designs of both the suppliers and the trucks. Some suppliers have modern, high-flow, computer-controlled loading systems, but many do not. Loading fuel at the various petroleum terminals is performed in either of two ways: top loading or bottom loading.

Top loading is the older method and calls for the fuel to be put into the cargo tanks through the dome covers on the top of the tank. While simple, top loading requires platforms at the loading facili-

ties from which people can get onto the trucks. Top loading takes longer than its alternative, since the person doing the loading has to walk to each compartment and dispense the fuel.

Bottom loading, by contrast, is quicker and is accomplished through the same lines on the cargo tank used for unloading. A special "dry-break" connection prevents fuel from leaking when the hoses are disconnected. All the controls on the cargo tank can be clustered together, too, allowing the loader to fill the entire tank from one area.

With or without high-tech loading equipment, most of today's tanker trucks have multiple prod- uct storage compartments, each of which features its own loading provisions, allowing multiple compartments to be loaded simultaneously with either similar or different products (for instance, one might contain premium grade gasoline, while another only regular grade). Contamination isn't a problem since tank construction prevents the fuel in one compartment from mixing with that in another. Even if an operator incorrectly leaves a small amount of one type of fuel in an "empty" tank, and that tank is then filled with a different type of fuel, there usually would not be a problem, since the residual fuel would be so diluted. For example, a few gallons of diesel fuel left in a tank would not present a problem if 9,000 gallons of gasoline were then loaded into the tank — the few gallons of diesel would be so diluted, it would be only a trace contamination per gallon of gas. Similarly, a small amount of gasoline left in a tank that is then filled with 7,700 gallons of diesel fuel would pose no contamination problems either.

Known as The Tootsie Roll Tanker, this Kenworth hauled fuel from Barstow, California, to Vernon, California, for Vernon Truck Wash, "Where Class is a Clean Truck."

Two low-mount Peterbilts, circa 1947, are seen in this 1967 photo. Smith Tank Lines ran a fleet of these older trucks well into the 1960s.

Large quantities, on the other hand, would contaminate a dissimilar fuel. Problems ranging from reduced power to engine damage could result.

Of course, tanks don't generally remain empty for very long. And when it comes to loading, at many of the more modern petroleum terminals, it can take as little as eight minutes to load 9,000 gallons of fuel! Add an extra few minutes for the necessary computer work, connecting and disconnecting the equipment, and signing the necessary highway transportation receipts and a tanker truck driver can be in and out of a loading station in under 15 minutes.

Similarly, unloading product at a retail gas station routinely takes 18 to 24 minutes, including "gauging" the station's underground tanks before and after delivery, protecting the unloading area with cones, unloading 9,000 gallons of gasoline in three grades, and getting the receipts signed.

As quickly as fuel can be unloaded at a gas station, the entire time carries with it a certain degree of risk. With motorists crowding the station's lot, poor station design and often precariously located

underground tanks there are ample opportunities for accidents to occur — and involve the tanker truck and its operator.

The fact that certain neighborhoods may not be as safe as others shouldn't be overlooked either, particularly because delivering gasoline is a 24-hours-a-day task. Try delivering in a high-crime area on a Friday or Saturday night, where gangs and drug trafficking abound, when you are the only one around conducting honest work, and you'll quickly learn the meaning of the term "vulnerable." And with most trucking companies frowning on drivers carrying weapons, it's easy to understand why most truckers try to simply unload as quickly and as safely as possible until they can get the hell out of there! And bear in mind that not all truck drivers are men, for whom such a situation can be scary enough.

Truck configurations for petroleum transportation are governed by state laws and where the equipment is based. Possible combinations include a double (a tractor and two trailers), a semi (a tractor and one trailer), and truck and trailer (a straight

This combination of trailers are called B-trains, and are quite popular in Canada. This Mack Superliner is operated by Mega Fuels in Williams Lake, British Columbia (Canada)

truck and tank body pulling a smaller trailer than a semi would pull).

Usually a tractor and one semi trailer are a little lighter than a truck and trailer. About 8,900 gallons can be hauled on a truck and trailer, whereas 9,000 to 9,100 gallons can be carried on a semi. This may depend on the kind of suspension that is on the tractor, though, since air suspension systems make for a heavier truck, which then necessitates a lighter cargo weight.

It's also interesting to note that the kind of fuel being hauled affects the weight of the vehicle, and thus how much fuel can be hauled. For example, aviation fuel is lighter than automobile gasoline, so as much as 200 more gallons of "av gas" can be hauled than automobile gas. On the other hand, jet fuel is little heavier than automobile gasoline, so only around 8,000 gallons can be carried. Diesel fuel is even heavier yet — only about 7,700 gallons can be transported.

The maximum cargo a truck can carry is a straightforward matter of subtracting the truck's (and trailer's) own weight from the state-specified combination weight (that of the truck, plus the trailer, plus the cargo). The truck's weight is measured when it is first put into service. The truck is weighed fully fueled and equipped with all necessary accessories, including safety devices. Using the typical specific gravity of each type of fuel, one can calculate the maximum quantity of each type of fuel that can be legally carried. Maximum combination weights for tankers differ from state to state. In California, 80,000 pounds is allowed for both a semi or a truck and trailer.

Interestingly, cargo volume varies with the temperature of the substance. For example, for every

five-degree increase in temperature, gasoline expands about 0.4 percent. Fuel suppliers bill their customers based on the gross quantity that was loaded, the specific gravity of the fuel, and its temperature when it went through the meter. Nine thousand gallons of unleaded gasoline loaded at 75 degrees and adjusted to 60 degrees would be billed as 9,034 gallons, because the fuel contracts when it cools. And just for your information, gasoline (motor gas and aviation gas) will evaporate and will also ignite at a lower temperature than will jet fuel (basically kerosene), diesel fuel or lube oil. That is the order of volatility for the forms of petroleum hauled. Jet fuel evaporates at a temperature that is lower than diesel fuel, but it is more stable than domestic gasoline.

Maximum cargo weights are just one of many safety measures that truckers must follow, and they're particularly important when dealing with transportation of petroleum products. A simple case in point is the occasional evening news story about a loaded gasoline tanker that was involved in an accident, began to leak, then was engulfed in a fire, and possibly resulted in multiple fatalities. (This sort of scenario, by the way, is by no means a common occurrence — it's purely a hypothetical example.) Actually, a properly maintained tank truck loaded with gasoline is no more dangerous than the person driving it. Yet accidents continue to occur as a result of motorists not knowing how to drive properly. Because a loaded gasoline tanker is heavier than an empty one, it is harder to stop. Also, if a tank is punctured or its structural integrity is compromised, then a loaded tanker is a bigger threat for the simple reason that it has a (usually) flammable substance inside that, under the right circumstances, could lead to a ferocious fire. An empty tanker, incidentally, is less of a threat because the vapors in the tank are generally too rich to burn (not enough oxygen). Besides, an empty tank truck is lighter, so it can stop and maneuver better to avoid accidents or react to erratic driving of other motorists.

As with most of the trucking vocations, the key safety factor in petroleum transport is proper driver training. Many of the larger oil companies and petroleum carriers employ the Smith System of Defensive Driving — a technique developed about 45 years ago that emphasizes avoiding situations that could require abrupt, emergency action by giving the driver time to see hazards as they develop, as well as to provide enough room to maneuver around them. The Smith System increases the driver's awareness level and teaches them to scan farther down the road, and beside them, for potential trouble. The system's five key steps are:

1 - Get the Big Picture
2 - Aim High in Steering
3 - Leave Yourself an Out
4 - Make Sure the Other Person Sees You
5 - Keep Your Eyes Moving

But because it's not always possible to avoid trouble, drivers are also trained how to properly control the truck if a situation does develop requiring quick, defensive action. It's necessary — even healthy — for the drivers to respect their cargo, but not necessarily to fear it.

The current systems under which petroleum products are transported have proven to be effective at preventing accidents. In fact, millions of gallons of gasoline are delivered every day without incident, yet this goes unreported because it doesn't make news. On the rare occasions when incidents do occur involving the handling of fuel, the incident is generally investigated to determine who and what was at fault.

Regardless of how safe a tanker operator may be, fuel spills and leaks can happen. Most of the larger oil companies have more stringent safety regulations than either the Environmental Protection Agency (EPA) or the Air Quality Management District (AQMD) require. These larger oil companies have policies and procedures in writing, which are given to each driver, instructing them on the proper handling of fuel. In addition, most state and federal agencies send inspectors to the various petroleum terminals to review the facilities, equipment, and procedures.

If, at the point of delivering gasoline to a local gas station, a small drip or small leak occurs, the driver can resolve the problem and perhaps only the AQMD might be notified. The fine would largely depend upon what the driver did, how fast he or she responded, what the impact was, plus the carrier's performance record with the AQMD. If, however, the spill was much bigger, or it wasn't cleaned up by the driver, the Regional Water Quality Control Board or EPA will become involved, because fuel could get into a waterway through the storm system or by seeping through the ground. The carrier's responsiveness to and responsibility for the incident may also have a bearing on how much the fine will be. In any case, negligence by the trucker or carrier can cost as much as $25,000 a day from the beginning of the incident until the cleanup is declared complete by the agency.

Beyond just the financial impact of spills, oil companies are also very much concerned about

Thunderbird Lubrications of Spokane, Washington, operates this twin-steering Peterbilt truck and trailer. Additional weight can be carried when there are more axles.

their public image. Again, the news media is quick to print negative publicity, such as the Exxon spill that occurred in 1989 in Alaska. But where are these newsreporters when a trucker gets praise from some motorist? Sadly, the good deeds of carriers and truckers go largely unreported.

In recent years, the larger oil companies have learned the value of a clean, good-looking tanker, driven in a safe manner by a professional, wearing a clean uniform with short hair and a positive personality. Most — if not all — petroleum companies insist that their drivers exhibit safety and road courtesy at all times. A clean truck, with a neat logo, combined with a driver that is well-groomed reinforces the public's image of a particular carrier or oil company. Most gas stations prefer to have their particular oil company deliver their products, as the company's hallmark and name stand out and this makes for good advertising. Likewise, truckers working for a particular oil company will tend to take more interest in delivering to stations that represent the same oil company for which they drive.

As was mentioned earlier, hauling gasoline in a semi may differ from that of a truck and trailer due mainly in the configuration of the gas stations. Many of these stations are built on smaller plots of land, so delivering gas or diesel fuel might be easier to perform in a truck and trailer due to greater maneuverability and flexibility and a tighter turning radius. However, a tractor and semi trailer may be less expensive to buy (a semi trailer costs about $40,000, not including the tractor or power unit). If

The few Dodge Bighorns that are still around are mostly shown at truck shows. Not so with this one, owned by Lanny Schooler of Daggett, California, who hauls gas and diesel fuel up and down Interstate 15 and Interstate 40 daily.

the tractor needs to be taken out of service for any reason, another tractor can be put under the semi trailer. Conversely, when a truck and trailer goes out of service, the entire unit is down.

Petroleum carriers face other special problems that most truckers are not encumbered with. For instance, petroleum carriers can't just park anywhere when it's time to eat. Unlike others in trucking, there are federal, state, and local laws that govern where and how a truck carrying hazardous materials is to be parked. Generally, most of the larger oil companies request that their drivers do not park their rigs loaded and they strongly prefer that the trucker stop to eat after his or her rig is unloaded.

As for servicing the trucks, schedules are usually dictated by both DOT requirements for the larger carriers and oil companies, plus the truck manufacturer's warranty requirements.

The trucking industry, like most other industries, has benefited from constant evolution. Newer, upgraded equipment has made life easier for employees of petroleum companies, while at the same time made those employees more productive. Perhaps the most important changes, equipment-wise, have been the development of the aluminum tank trailer and body, plus the on-truck vapor recovery systems.

One of the advantages of using aluminum to construct tanks was mentioned earlier — that it is

Tri Valley Distributing of Utah, hauls petroleum using triple tanks for maximum payload. This kind of configuration is legal in most of the western states. Seen here is a Kenworth complete with a 36-inch sleeper.

less likely to spark in an accident. But aluminum has another benefit, too: it weighs less than steel. Because aluminum trailers and tanks are lighter than their steel counterparts, greater payloads to be transported, which translates into increased profit potential for the carriers and oil companies per load. So, using aluminum trailers is not only a safer choices, but a more financially sound one, as well.

The second big change in equipment is that of vapor recovery systems, which trap environmentally hazardous vapors that, until recently, were allowed to simply vent to the atmosphere around us. This change lessens the impact that petroleum products have on our environment.

Each of these changes underscore the fact that safety is the name of the game for today's successful petroleum carriers and the oil companies. Like most of us, the carriers and oil producers are concerned about the environment in which we live, so they take every precaution — many voluntary, some legislated — to prevent spills or other damage that may be caused by the production or transportation of petroleum products, because although petroleum comes from the ground, it often cannot return to this ground without causing some sort of ecological damage.

An example of such precautions is that truckers who haul petroleum have to comply with not only all the laws that pertain to operating a commercial vehicles, but they must also comply with hazardous materials regulations that don't apply to others in the trucking industry, such as rules that dictate where and how far tankers must park from each other and other structures, how often the vehicles must be checked en route to their delivery points, what the driver must do should an emergency occur, and that individuals are prohibited from smoking in or near the petroleum transportation vehicles.

Furthermore, the larger oil companies may require vehicle safety inspections every 21 days — more frequent than the DOT's requirements that tanks and trucks carrying fuel be inspected every 28 days. On top of that, many states' air resources boards require annual inspections to check for tank integrity, plus an even more stringent inspection every five years. Integrity inspections are generally performed by the tank body or trailer manufacturer at their facilities.

Another regulation requires all hazardous materials haulers to have placards on their vehicles denoting what the hazard level is of their cargo — the lower the number on the placard, the higher the level of hazard. The HazMat code system was developed to comply with the United Nation's Hazard Communication program, so the same numbered code means the same in Canada, Mexico, or any

Pray At The Pump?

An old petroleum haulers tale is true, but of little concern today.

Some petroleum truckers advise that you should never put gasoline into your car's fuel tank when gasoline is being delivered to the station's underground tanks. Their reasoning, is that while you are pumping gas into your vehicle, sediment or water may be stirred up in the underground tanks as new gas is pumped in. The sediment could then be pumped into your vehicle's gas tank as you are pumping your gas.

In reality, problems such as what are described are largely just bad memories. Most of the major oil companies maintain their underground tanks and can't afford the bad publicity that can go with contaminated fuel. So, most tank pumps feature filters to screen out contaminants, plus fuel dispensers have their own filters, too, that further prevent contaminants from entering your car's fuel tank. However, you should still be cautious of the "cheap" stations that advertise inexpensive gasoline — you may pay for it later in the form of an engine overhaul or fuel injection system repairs.

Even if contaminants do get into your vehicle's fuel tank, your car draws it through its own filter that will catch all but the tiniest remaining particles. Still, a good rule of thumb is that if the gas station is clean and spotless, then there should be no problem with its gas, even if there is a new delivery at the time you are pumping gas into your vehicle. If, however, the gas station is unorganized and appears dirty, then the gas that you pump may also reflect this condition.

other nation. A Hazardous Materials Guide lists all the codes, the hazard classes, descriptions of the materials and their hazards, and how to respond to them in an emergency.

A common HazMat placard seen quite frequently is for gasoline (or gasohol), which is identified by the number 1203, which means that the liquid is flammable and that fire is its greatest danger. It can get into your skin or in your mouth but such contact may not be serious, provided that you flush the area with water immediately.

Two different numbers identify diesel fuel: 1202 or 1993, while jet fuel may have the number 1863.

Both diesel and jet fuels take more heat to ignite than does conventional gasoline, and they are not likely to be too harmful if they come in contact with skin or are swallowed, again provided the area of contact is flushed with plenty of water. Any vehicle loaded with a hazardous material must have a placard on each side and on the end of the container (tank), so a semi will have at least four placards (in most cases, a placard is installed on the front of the tractor, as well). A truck and trailer rig would have at least six placards for the entire unit.

Not all changes within the petroleum hauling field are safety motivated, however. It should come as a surprise to no one that carriers and oil companies alike are always on the lookout for a new way to save a few dollars, further maximize efficiency, or increase business.

One recent innovation that carriers have found appealing comes courtesy of the tire manufacturers, in the form of new "super-single" or "wide-base" tires on light-weight aluminum wheels. The big advantage here is that super-single tires and wheels save about 300 pounds per axle, and as we discussed earlier, the more vehicle weight is saved, the more cargo weight can be increased, and the more money can be made off each load. Super-singles also allow carriers to maintain a smaller inventory of spare tires and wheels (after all, each truck has half as many wheels per axle). While use of super-singles continues, a few drawbacks have been gleaned from their use thus far. First, super-singles are not compatible with the standard dual tires and wheels found on most trucks, so super-singles and duals can't be mixed and matched. Second, when a super-single tire decides to go flat, a replacement has to be delivered to the truck as quickly as possible, since petroleum-carrying tankers cannot be moved.

Tire manufacturers are also to thank for another new technology that is currently being tried and evaluated by the trucking industry: low profile or "low rider" tires. These lighter and smaller tires come with a reduced price tag, plus their smaller size increases stability by lowering the truck's center of gravity. They even increase payload capacity. But again, all is not roses. Low rider tires suffer a reduced tire life, thanks in part to the simple fact that the smaller tires travel at least 73 more revolutions per mile than their standard 22-1/2-inch counterparts over a one mile stretch of road. Low rider tires also reduce clearances, which increases the potential for getting "high centered" at a railroad crossing or other obstacle.

Smaller oil companies, such as United Oil Co., often take as much — if not more — pride in their equipment as do larger companies. This 1988 Peterbilt is a living tribute to the smaller companies, proud to serve the motoring public.

The future of hauling petroleum appears pretty positive, despite threats from several alternative energy sources.

Electricity, for instance, has a long way to go — especially in terms of practicality — before the public will accept it as an alternative source of automotive power, even if it is mandated by the federal government. There are, simply, too many "bugs" to be worked out, still, and many of their solutions are a long way from being resolved. And electricity is just too expensive to be an attractive option for heating a home.

Natural gas, another alternative, has not proven effective for heavy hauling, since it cannot produce the BTU's (British Thermal Units, a measurement of heat, and thus power) that diesel fuel can. Natural gas also does not offer the convenience of gasoline or diesel fuel, either.

In the end, petroleum hauling provides a vital service for businesses and consumers, alike. And though there are inherent dangers in transporting petroleum products for the truck operators, there are few forms of cargo that are more easily loaded or dispensed than those lucrative liquids that simply flow in and out, without any heavy lifting.

Chapter 5

Flatbed and Oversize Loads
Turning Heads Wherever They go

Nothing catches people's attention quicker than seeing some humungous load, a mobile or modular home or a huge piece of construction equipment being trucked down an interstate on a flatbed or lowbed trailer. Heads turn as the escort vehicles lead and/or follow these huge loads, with their amber roof lights warning others of an unusual size cargo that may impact normal travel patterns.

Whatever the massive load is that they're hauling, these oversize loads — whether that means extra tall, extra wide, extra long, or extra heavy — are not the everyday, run-of-the-mill kind of cargo, and that catches people's attention.

Moving the unusual takes a lot of skill, patience, and experience. Aside from the obvious challenges in transporting an oversize load, the trucker should know a little about rigging and carpentry, plus a good deal about the limits of what his or her equipment can do.

As those in the business know, transporting an oversize load also involves considerable planning and preparation. Aside from assembling the necessary people and equipment to safely handle the job of moving an oversize load, there are various permits that must be obtained from the cities, counties, and states that may be impacted by such loads. For example, an oversize load covering only a 20-mile distance, may include jurisdictions of as many

Hauling humongous loads presents no special problems for this highway-heavyweight, a Peterbilt pulling for Bill Signs Trucking of El Cajon, California.

Tarps are necessary to protect the cargo, especially if the weather calls for rain and the load is cardboard. Pictured in this 1981 photo is a 1950 Kenworth high-mount, owned by Jansen Transportation of La Puente, California.

as a dozen different governmental agencies, most — if not all — of which require separate permits.

For interstate moves of oversize loads, even more permits may be necessary in order to comply with all of the local, state, and federal laws. Generally, permits are required for loads that exceed a gross weight of 80,000 pounds or more, or measure over 102 inches in width, or over 13 feet, 6 inches high. Permits are generally obtained at departments of motor vehicle, truck scales, Ports of Entries at each state, or regional offices within a city or county having governmental facilities.

Costs of getting the various permits can range from as little as $15 to several thousand dollars, depending on what jurisdictions are involved, depending on the weight of the load, its dimensions, the length or duration of the move, and what routes are to be taken. Obviously, this cost is included in the total bill for moving such a load. Large moves may take many months to get all of the permits, because the safest routes of travel must be planned in advance, engineers must be consulted to determine the strength of bridges

along the route, plus the best time for the transporting must be carefully considered before permits are issued.

To move a special permit load without getting the proper permits and written approval would be like walking in an uncharted mine field. If a carrier was caught without the necessary permits, the fines and penalties could be high enough to put them right out of business. Ports of Entries, various scales, tollway employees, highway patrols, and other law enforcement agencies have the authority to cite and, in extreme cases, arrest those people moving a special load without proper documentation, too.

Different states have different requirements on how many pilot or escort vehicles must accompany the load during transport, and states are beginning to certify the various companies engaged in providing pilot car services, in an effort to ensure public safety.

There seems to be no uniformity among the states regarding what special equipment may be required for the trucks that carry oversize loads.

Permits

Depending on the type of cargo being hauled and the specific route to be taken, truckers may find themselves in the uncomfortable position of having to obtain numerous permits from multiple states, many counties, and other officials. Typical of most bureaucracies, the process is almost never handled the same way by any two officials, and the permits required are almost never quite the same.

While there is still a great deal of progress to be made in simplifying the process of making sure a trucker has all the necessary permits to legally transport cargo, many improvements have been made over the past 20 years by the Specialized Carriers & Rigging Association, a part of the American Trucking Association. Annual symposiums, hosted by SCERA, bring together state permit officials to seek solutions to common problems and identify uniformity issues. There may still be work to be done, but the steps taken so far are welcome ones.

Some states ask for one amber flashing light, located on the roof of the tractor that is pulling the trailer(s), while other states may insist on two amber lights situated on a different part of the tractor. There is no standard placement for such lights. And, when hauling loads across state lines, carriers need to make sure they meet the requirements of each state — plus any special county or even city or town requirements.

Other equipment used on flatbed, stepdeck, and oversize loads include the proper number of chains and binders needed to safely secure the load to the trailer, to prevent the load from shifting or moving while it is in transit. Some states even specify how many chains and binders must be used, depending on the type of cargo, its size and weight. In addition, the federal Department of Transportation's Bureau of Motor Carrier Safety (BMCS), dictates how a load must be secured and the specific strength of both chains and binders are defined. The various states and provinces operate under the umbrella of the Commercial Vehicle Safety Alliance (CVSA), which enforces the securement rules and has been instrumental in advocating stricter en-

Loads that are over-width, shown in this picture, require special permits. These permits spell out, exactly, what routes to take and what hours of travel can be used.

Previous Page
Ron Salvador's 1949 high-mount Peterbilt is seen here in Oregon. Straps are used in securing loads like this one. Tying down a load like this presents no special problems.

ment devices.

Tarps are another valuable item that may be needed to insure that the cargo or load won't be damaged or destroyed by rain, snow, strong winds, or blowing sand. These tarps, in past times, were made of heavy canvas because canvas resists moisture and protects against strong winds. Certain items must be kept dry, such as cardboard boxes, building materials (bagged cement, drywall, lumber), and canvas provides this margin of safety. More recently, tarps have been made of lighter materials, like plastic, which is easier to work with and can provide better protection in many cases. While it is still common to see tarps loosely secured, blowing in the wind, careful folding and securing by the driver, plus innovations in fasteners are making tarping more and more like a giant form of gift-wrapping every day — including pretty wrapping, since most tarps now proudly and prominently feature the carriers logo for added advertisement and recognition.

State and local laws are generally adopted from federal law in terms of mandated safety devices, and it's up to the states to enforce those laws. In many states, straps may be acceptable for tying down loads, such as in the case of transporting lumber. Again, federal law dictates how strong

Tarps and straps are used to secure this flatbed load. Over-The-Hill Trucking, based in Oregon, owns this neat-looking 1959 Kenworth. In 1959, Kenworth offered a Fiberglas front end that tilted, as an option. This KW has the traditional butterfly hood.

these straps must be. When hauling hay or alfalfa, certain types of rope are approved but, again, they must meet strict standards of strength.

At times, it seems the United States is "united" in name only. When it comes to moving flatbed and oversize loads, a 12-foot extension or overhang may be legal in one state, but illegal in another. The same may be true of loads that protrude from the sides or front of a trailer. As a result, commodities that are over 14-feet wide may present a special challenge if the final destination is 3,000 miles cross-country.

Beyond public safety, there are laws to protect the load's driver, as well. Federal regulations require that flatbed, stepdeck, and lowbed trailers have a headboard, or that the tractor hauling

This 1966 photo shows an over-length load being pulled by a Peterbilt cab-over that's owned by Owl Truck and Construction of Los Angeles.

Mounting or repairing one of these tires is not a job for the auto club to perform. Because these tires are lying flat, the center of gravity is less. Thus a safer load is assured with proper straps holding the load in place

them have a "headache rack." Either device is intended to prevent cargo from crashing through the back of the truck cab should the cargo come loose and slide forward.

Oversize loads can present special challenges, and thus can have special requirements. One such requirement stipulates the red flags on all four corners of the load to attract people's attention, alerting them to use caution around it. In addition to flags, red lights are required for night and early morning moves when the flags wouldn't be readily visible; however, exact placement of the lights may differ from state to state. Stepdeck or single-drop trailers, as well as double-drop or lowbed trailers, have different configurations where the deck or platform of the trailer is much closer to the ground. Stepdeck trailers are necessary when loads of more than 19 feet high are transported. Hauling over-height loads brings with it special problems. If the load is heavy, as in the case of moving an electrical transformer, the center of gravity is made higher, making it a sensitive job when it comes to making turns. Also, low bridges have to be considered, as the "scalping" of a load may occur if the bridge is too low. For this reason, preplanning the route is

a must. Also, there are traffic signals that hang low, telephone and electrical wires that need to be addressed before going down the highway. Hauling any load that exceeds 15 feet high, overall, and consists of a coast-to-coast move may be the load that "separates the men from the boys."

Hauling an over-height item may be especially challenging because such loads are often top-heavy. Over-wide loads tend to be side-heavy making them a bit tricky to haul. Anytime the weight of an object is being transported is off-center or otherwise displaced, there is the potential for "surprise" movements.

Weather plays an important role when oversize moves are being contemplated, too. Rain, sleet, or snow will generally "ground" any movement of such loads. For this reason, sunny, dry, and clear conditions are preferred by most truckers who move oversize cargo — the job is hard enough without fighting Mother Nature, as well.

Realistically, of course, aside from hauling "post-holes," there are no easy loads for flatbed-type trailers. Still, any load that is both easy to secure or tie down and doesn't require additional time or effort to resecure during transit is an ideal load. From time to time, you'll see obviously heavy loads being pulled down the interstates by multi-axle configurations. Because of the additional axles, the weight of the load is distributed over a greater area, so that there is no damage to the highways due to overweight. In fact, most oversize loads do not exert any more weight per square inch of tire contact patch, than do regular loads that do not need permits.

All the special planning, permits, equipment, and attention needed for transportation of oversize loads naturally makes such shipments more costly than other types of freight hauling. But most oversize load haulers aren't in it for the money — the profits aren't generally much greater than those earned for hauling multiple loads totaling a similar weight. Instead, many truckers enjoy the unusual nature of the job and the special thought that must be put into the project, which helps keep things interesting. And the fact that they can make fewer runs than many other truckers to earn a comparable living is generally a nice bonus that really pays off in terms of more family or free time.

This photo, taken in Hawaii in 1975, shows an off-highway model Kenworth loaded to the "max" with sugar cane. Semis this size are seldom seen in public, as they generally operate on backroads and private property. Other applications for this size of truck can include oil field work and logging operations. A 12V71 Detroit Diesel engine, backed by an automatic transmission supplies the muscle for this sugar-hauler.

Chapter 6

The Bullhaulers

The Old West Meeting Modern Technology

Many truckers tend to think of themselves as "The Last American Cowboy." Most of these cowboy wannabes are hauling freight or liquid loads. But if any trucker truly deserves to be compared to that American icon, the cowboy, then surely it would be those guys and gals that haul livestock. Livestock haulers are about the closest thing to actual cowboys today, and livestock truckers are a breed all their own.

Aside from the obvious hazards of passing a loaded livestock rig, the levels of danger can range from the comical to downright deadly!

On the lighthearted end of things is the fact that "animal exhaust residue" can spray out of one of the many slats or vent-holes alongside the body or trailer of the rig, predictably soiling whatever stands between the animal and the ground, be it an open-top Porsche convertible, a motorcycle cop, or another trucker. For this reason, livestock truckers tend to park away from the "rest of the herd" at truck stops. They've found they make fewer enemies that way.

And hauling four-legged critters is not for tenderfoots, or crybabies either. Quite the contrary: Hauling livestock is, perhaps, one of the most complicated and demanding jobs for a trucker. While others may complain about having to load and un-

A Kenworth cab-over, an LT Mack, and a Sterling-White pose together at a ranch in Sierraville, California. This is how livestock trucks looked in the 1950s. Jim Dobbas owns the orange Kenworth, as well as the yellow Mack. Bruce and June Thomas are the owners of the red Sterling.

In this 1956 picture, we see a "Cherrypicker" International truck and trailer. This rig was owned by Ernie Falen of Caldwell, Idaho, and could haul cattle one way, and produce on its return. Trailers and bodies were steam-cleaned, prior to loading the produce. This was quite popular in the 1950s.

load their truck, a livestock hauler's job is a combination of trucker, lion tamer, veterinarian, and rancher, requiring fast reflexes, a dull sense of smell and the ability to estimate the weight of the livestock that is being carried, since overweight fines are not cheap. An experienced livestock hauler tries to plan ahead on both loading and moving his rig down the highways.

Livestock hauling is generally performed in truck and trailer rigs (a straight truck with a body, pulling another trailer less than 30 feet long), a set of doubles (a tractor pulling two trailers), or as a semi (tractor and one trailer, generally about 53 feet long). Most of the semi trailers are either straight-deck in design or the more popular "possum-belly" or pot trailers. The latter is designed to carry more animals than the straight-deck type of trailer. Newer trailers are longer and wider, making it "max out" on weight before they run out of

room. Too much room aboard a livestock trailer will cause to load to shift or move while being transported on roads that have tight turns or steeply crowned roads, possibly leading to disasterous results. Sudden stops or quick turning can seriously injure or bruise animals that were otherwise in good condition at the start of a trip — and that usually ends up costing the carrier money. And such concerns are only intensified with double-deck trailers, which also run a high risk of rolling over, given their high center of gravity and unstable load. Livestock haulers must be constantly on guard to avoid sudden stopping or swerving — defensive driving must be the order of the day at all times.

Ironically, though, the toughest part of a livestock haulers job may just be during times when the truck isn't even moving, when the animals — be they cattle, sheep, goats, hogs, horses, or whatever

— are being loaded and unloaded. The skills and experience needed to coerce various living creatures on and off trailers aren't taught in books or schools — they're learned through trial and error, by doing them. And often that means doing them wrong first, then learning from your mistakes . . . hopefully quickly.

The first lesson to be learned is that every animal has a personality all its own. Cattle can kick you or run you over with deadly results. "Wood Blind" sheep can drive a trucker to drinking, because these critters just don't even know what they are trying to do. Hogs in confinement can be the most dangerous animals, because they have an "attitude" problem and resist any attempts to move them. And horses, especially high-spirited ones, may simply refuse to be loaded, and when a 1,500-pound animal doesn't want to be loaded, it takes a special kind of livestock handler to convince them otherwise.

To make loading and unloading the animals as easy as possible, many ranchers build loading ramps or chutes. The problem is, many ranchers often build these devices without thinking of the truckers who have to use them. For instance, wide chutes and big cattle generally don't work well for the smaller and younger calves, which will have the room to turn around while they are being loaded. Beyond that, many of the chutes are made of wood and may be in dire need of major repairs, having been eaten away by termites. Given all the tasks that demand a rancher's time and money, it's not too surprising that their loading chutes and ramps fall victim to the same old story: they'll fix it next year. It should be noted that not all ranchers have poorly maintained ramps or chutes, some even go to the expense to make their loading facilities of steel or aluminum.

Generally, loading or unloading at a feedlot is a lot easier than at independent ranches, though, because the loading chutes and ramps are designed by people who know the problems experienced by the livestock haulers.

Worse than the ranches, however, are the packing plant chutes, which usually seem to have been designed by people who have never loaded livestock before, according to some seasoned cattle haulers.

A Kenworth, circa 1965, is seen here pulling for E.B. Manning & Son of Pico Rivera, California. For many years, the Manning Kenworths were the cleanest cattle trucks on the highway. Manning prides itself on offering only the finest meat to gourmet restaurants and upscale markets.

A few of the trucks operated by Fred Whitehead are seen in this 1967 picture. Truck and trailer livestock trucks were quite a common sight in the West.

Other loading and unloading obstacles abound, too. A classic problem is that sheep can be hard to load when the sun is bright and in their eyes. The solution would seem obvious then — load them at night. But bright lights spook them, too. Dimmer night lights, placed in the proper positions, can aid in loading during the evenings.

Cattle make an excellent example of how complicated transporting livestock can be. For one thing, there are different types of cattle. Fat cattle can be 1,000 to 1,300 pounds, so a trucker must be accurate in counting how many of these heavier cattle are loaded, if he or she hopes to avoid overweight fines. These fat cattle are usually trucked to kill plants or slaughterhouses.

Feeder cattle can weigh from 700 to 900 pounds, and are generally transported to feedlots so they can be fattened up. Lighter and younger calves go to "warm up" feedlots, where they are fed a mixture of hay and grain, before being move to the feedlots that serve "hotter" mixes of cattle feed.

"Springer" or dairy cattle, ready to calve, are moved to milk barns. Calves and their mother cows have to be separated in transit, since the younger calves can be trampled by the larger cows. Inside the trailers there are gates and dividers to separate younger animals from being pushed, shoved, and trampled by their more aggressive elders.

In hauling livestock, the cargo must be checked from time to time, in order to insure that all the animals are standing on all "fours." Animals packed into a tight area can get a bit impatient, to say the least, and if the temperature is in the triple digits, cattle can suffocate, or they can get trampled to death in a matter of minutes in any weather. Experienced livestock haulers will check their load after

Seen driving out of a truck wash is this sharp-looking Freightliner, owned by S&T Trucking of Wyoming. Livestock trucks have come a long way since the old wooden racks of the 1930s to 1960s.

Seen here in a 1956 photo at the Los Angeles Union Stock-yards is a 1940s Kenworth cab-over truck and trailer owned by Garibaldi Bros. Starting in 1933, Garibaldi was the largest hauler of livestock in the 11 western states. Colors for the Garibaldi equipment included dark green racks, with dark blue cabs and red frames and wheels.

the first 30 minutes of loading and every 1-1/2 to 2 hours after that to make sure all is well.

Livestock, like most humans, don't do well in extremely hot or cold weather. Keeping your truck moving is the name of the game in sheep hauling in hot weather, because the air ventilation coming in tends to cool them through their wool "coats." Hauling hogs in the winter requires that side panels be in place in order to prevent loss of body heat, but in the summer, hogs have to be cooled down with a special water system found in many livestock trailers.

As for the number of animals that can be hauled in an average 53-foot possum belly or pot trailer really depends on what kind of animal is being hauled, and what the legal weight is for the particular state that the equipment is operating in. Each state has different weight restrictions or requirements. Several states allow for a gross weight of 105,000 pounds. That is 35,000 unladen (weight of the truck), plus 70,000 pounds for the load. A 47-foot livestock trailer can "max out" in an 80,000 pound state, so there would be no advantage to pulling a 53-foot trailer then.

On a truck and trailer setup, with a 27-foot aluminum body, pulling a 27-foot aluminum pot trailer, a typical load can consist of over 500 lambs, triple-decked on the truck, and quadrupled on the pull trailer. If the load of lambs is 53,000 pounds, and the weight of the truck and trailer is 27,000 (empty) then the gross weight would be 80,000 pounds, making it legal in most of the western

states. If the pull trailer has a spread axle configuration, then an additional 4,000 pounds can be gained in some of the western states.

Because all animals are not equal, a trucker has to tailor his or her methods to suit the type of animal being hauled. In many cases, some truckers specialize in hauling one type of animal or another; they may have been trained in hauling sheep but not cattle. It's also helpful if a trucker's personality compliments that of the load he's carrying. For example, truckers with "short-fuses" (bad tempers) aren't particularly well-suited to hauling sheep — a hot-tempered driver could wind up proving that the sheep are smarter than the trucker! On the other hand, if a trucker is intimidated by the size of fat cattle or large bulls, they may be afraid of being kicked or trampled by these larger bovines and so may prefer to haul sheep or hogs, because they're smaller.

Large bulls present a clear and present danger in loading and unloading . . . just give them room and respect! Experienced cattle haulers, however, will give even greater caution to the old cow that just came out of the desert country, as many of them have not seen a human on foot, nor know what a fence or a big rig is. As a result, a smaller, wild and woolly desert cow can "nail" a trucker to the inside wall of his trailer, if this trucker is not aware of the dangers in loading this unique animal.

Of course, some truckers believe that it's easier to haul sheep than cattle. If properly loaded and the initial check of the load is okay, sheep will give less of a problem. It's in the unloading that determines who is experienced and who is a "Tenderfoot." "Woolblind" sheep (because of the wool growing over their eyes), are harder to load and unload. Lambs can pile up like cotton candy, and sometimes a good sheep dog will work better than the trucker hauling the load. In most cases, hauling sheep requires a lot of patience on the part of the trucker.

Unlike many trucking fields, hauling livestock, like hauling hay, tends to develop a closeness that bonds people together. It's part of the country mentality — that everybody pitches in to help each other, even truckers who work for competing outfits. A rancher may drive many miles out of the way in order to show a trucker where a given ranch can be found. This may mean many miles off of a paved highway. In earlier times, a livestock trucker, looking for a ranch 50 miles off an interstate, could rely on nearby residents to assist in getting to a given location. However, with technology making inroads, a cellular phone makes things a lot easier. If the driver gets a phone number for his destination,

This 1967 picture was taken in Tucson, Arizona, at the Triple T Truck Stop, owned by Ira Morris. The cattle rig in this picture was owned by Tommie Harris of Agua Dulce, Texas, and the trailer is a 40-footer.

he can always call from the road for those sometimes intricate last directions.

Yes, livestock truckers are a clannish breed. They tend to stay together, and as was mentioned, other truckers tend to complain, when "animal exhaust residue" flies out of the livestock trailer and on to their shiny "large cars." And speaking of flies, they, too, come with the territory. Hauling livestock without the annoyance of flies would be like ordering a Rolls Royce and not getting air conditioning. The flies are everywhere, they get into everything, and they're yet another reason livestock haulers tend to stick together.

While there may not be much that can be done about the fly situation, livestock hauling has benefited from several quite obvious advances over the past 40 years. From the 1920s to the early 1970s, livestock bodies and trailers were made of wood. But a wood-bodied cattle truck and trailer of the 1950s could weigh in at 40,000 pounds empty, with only 48 feet of loading capacity. Obviously, this added a lot of unnecessary weight to a semi or truck and trailer rig. Aluminum, on the other hand, solved the weight problem plus lasts considerably longer, so today a livestock truck with 84 feet of loading space — nearly double the old wooden trucks — can weigh in at only 26,000 pounds — almost half that of the wooden trucks of yesteryear. The weight savings of aluminum was dramatic allowing both bigger trucks and trailers, as well as additional cargo capacity.

There had been some doubts on the part of the ranchers, feedlot folks, and meat packers about the use of aluminum livestock bodies and trailers. There was natural skepticism, with ranchers, packers, and the feedlot personnel wondering how the animals could be unloaded after they were herded into these new "tin boxes," as they were called. Besides, they reasoned, if cattle with large horns were loaded, their horns would tear up the sides, making the aluminum bodies look like sardine cans. All of these myths proved not to have any validity.

Still, for all its advantages, aluminum is vulnerable to the acids in animal waste, which can eat through both wood and aluminum, if not properly removed. These acids can attack both the floors and the sides, as well as all the moving parts (doors, gates, ramps) found on the trailer or truck body. Standard procedure after a haul is a good cleaning, though, so this is not generally a great concern.

On the subject of ramps, gates, and doors, each have received vast improvements, eliminating the need for double-deck chutes found at ranches and feedlots.

Regardless of what they haul, most trucks try to get backloads — loads for the return trip to home — to be profitable. This isn't always the case, but if a trucker is hauling hogs into California, then he or she may try to get a load of feeder cattle back to Colorado, Kansas, or Nebraska. Then, perhaps, some fat cattle to Iowa. This depends, of course, on whether the livestock hauling operation is geared to hauling long distance loads and is licensed to run in the various states.

Hauling sheep generally may pay more, because the cost of setting up deckboards for sheep and hogs comes into play. Aluminum boards cost an average of $25 each, and more bedding is needed for sheep and hogs. A bag of wood shavings, to absorb animal waste and prevent slippery footing, is about $6 a bag.

As we touched on earlier, if an animal is bruised or dies in transit, the carrier must bear the responsibility. Therefore, a detailed check of each animal loaded is absolutely essential. All bruised or injured animals should be noted and written on the freight bill before moving the herd, so that the trucker is not held responsible for preexisting injuries. In times past, several packing plants used to discount freight bills with false claims of animal bruising. However, after many complaints by the carriers, the Public Utilities Investigators brought a halt to this practice. Nevertheless, the loss of one animal in transit, can wipe out any profit that would have been made for the entire load.

Speaking of dead animals, there used to be a demand for them, when dead animals were recycled

Morosa Bros. of Bakersfield, California ran a fleet of mixed livestock trucks. Seen here in this 1957 picture is a Peterbilt cab-over, circa 1951, with sleeper cab. Wood bodies on trucks and trailers prevailed during the 1950s.

into by-products by the rendering plants. Because of newer regulations on feeding these by-products back to the animals, demand has declined to the point where there is now often a cost in some areas to remove and dispose of these animals.

The future of the livestock haulers is uncertain and may be up for grabs. Truckers in the business of hauling livestock are on-call 24 hours a day, seven days a week. In addition to working in an environment where the aroma can clear "a mother-in-law's sinus a mile away," there is always the forces of "Murphy's Law" working against the trucker. Clean clothes that are supposed to last for up to three days, may be "baptized" with animal waste 15 minutes after first putting them on.

Far more serious, however, is the problem of finding qualified drivers. Young wives want their husbands home with them at night, and the smell of Texas Longhorns sharing the same bed with them isn't exactly the best romantic setting. A lot

of the younger farm kids these days want jobs with set 9:00 to 5:00 hours. And inexperienced drivers can run off customers, especially hauling sheep.

On top of that, the DOT is giving greater attention to hours of driving, because the concern for the care of the livestock can force a driver to drive extra hours just to complete the delivery of the cargo in good condition and in good time.

And if all of this weren't enough, the various animal rights groups are becoming more vocal in their cries of over-crowded livestock trailers, poor animal care on the road, and other allegations.

These issues have, predictably, had a financial impact on the livestock industry, which, to say the least, has seen better days. One cause of these harder times could be because of the medical profession's recent statements that encourage people to eat less meat and more vegetables and fruits. Gone are the days when motorists out West read the "Eat Western Beef" signs that adorned the backs of cattle trailers. Because of this financial slump, rates for hauling livestock are difficult to increase, which means more and more livestock haulers are having to make do on less and less income, and that's hardly a formula for long-term prosperity and success.

However, bullhaulers are a tough breed and they have seen this many times before. They are survivors and many are well able to "ride" the current downward trend out, waiting for better days to return.

Hauling livestock brings the romance of the Old West into focus with today's big rigs. To many people, the aroma of animal waste (especially in cattle hauling), blended with the smell of Number 2 diesel fuel, is the macho man's version of Georgio of Beverly Hills. If the "Last American Cowboy" is the trucker, then surely he's a livestock hauler. They're the only ones with the cowboy spirit, the cowboy drive, and the cowboy character.

A GMC cab-over truck and trailer owned by Talley Livestock Transportation of Madera, California, can be seen in this picture.

Chapter 7

Hay and Alfalfa Hauling

Keeping the Cows Happy

An old saying says to "make hay while the sun shines," but when it comes to hauling the stuff — and a similar product, alfalfa — it's a round-the-clock operation. There are lots of hungry animals out there depending on truckers to transport the stuff to ranches, farms, and feed stores all across the country.

Depending on where you live, hauling hay may conjure up a completely different image than it may in another region of the country. In the Midwest, for example, hauling hay consists of moving large round spools of the stuff on flatbed or lowbed trailers. But in the western parts of the country, alfalfa and hay are more typically found in bales or more rectangular shapes. This chapter will deal with the baled type, and will cover the various combinations of trucks and trailers used to transport this product.

In the West, there are basically two types of hauling hay and alfalfa. The traditional way may take more than an hour to physically place each load or bale into the correct position on a truck and trailer, a semi, or set of doubles. Each individual bale may weight up to 125 pounds, and an average load-count can be around 426 bales on a truck and trailer rig.

Ideally, if all goes well and there are no other truckers waiting to load, a little over one hour is needed to load and secure the load . . . that's if all goes well!

Early sunrise finds Ed Bonestroo and his 400-horsepower 1946 Autocar leaving Imperial Valley with this hay-squeeze load destined for some dairy in the Ontario/Chino area of California.

EDS 46 BONES TOY

Originally, this Peterbilt was a petroleum hauler for Golden Bear Marketing. Dean Berg, the driver, quit Golden Bear and purchased the truck. After converting it into a hay hauler, Dean and Linda Kangrga started their own business as Harvest Hay Company of Fontana, California.

Unlike many other forms of trucking, loading and unloading hay and alfalfa relies heavily upon manual labor, and so it should come as no surprise that both loading and unloading generally take roughly the same amount of time to accomplish. Unless you're a "pro" and use leverage over brute strength to place each of the more than 400 bales onto the truck, you'll know that you had your day's workout.

The second western method of hauling hay or alfalfa, the hay squeeze, has replaced the largely re-placed the traditional way of loading bales of hay. The hay squeeze bales are much larger and weigh in at about 1,800 pounds per bale. Needless to say,

one cannot physically move one of these by hand, so equipment similar to a large forklift does the loading, placing, and unloading . . . all of which can take less than 30 minutes to complete. Securing the load may also take less time than securing the 400-plus bales placed by hand, the old-fashioned way.

As with livestock haulers, hay haulers share a special relationship with their fellow hay haulers. It's not unusual to see one trucker helping another from a competing company. It's a closeness most other forms of trucking haven't seen since the 1940s, but happily, in hay hauling, everyone seems to pitch in and help each other out, because this is more than just a 9:00 to 5:00 job.

This is a 1948 "A" Model GMC owned by Bert Van Dyk of Ontario, California. This rig has appeared at many of the inter- and intrastate truck shows.

Like all of trucking, hauling hay and alfalfa has its share of problems. One major problem is the waiting — hay haulers don't get paid by the hour, but rather by the load. As a result, delays up to several hours can and do occur. This is especially true if there are several trucks ahead of yours, and the person unloading is new and lacks the experience to quickly unload a truck. Aside from unexpected or unscheduled periods of waiting, pulling a loaded big rig with hay can be quite tricky and downright hazardous if you don't know what you are doing. A high center of gravity and dense weight make the trucks handling potentially erratic, while strong winds, thick fog, careless motorists, and other factors only add to the unpredictability, ensuring that

this is a profession that's just not for the faint of heart. After all, stopping and especially turning has to be performed with the utmost of care, or the entire load will flip over and be dumped.

Because feed-quality hay and alfalfa must remain dry to prevent mold from growing and spoiling the products, the best time for hauling this commodity is generally from spring to the early winter months — periods that typically see less fog, wind, and rain. However, loading hay in Westmoreland, California, in July is no "piece of cake," with temperatures that can routinely climb to well over 110 degrees. The term "sweating to the oldies" takes on a whole new meaning! It's hot, the bales are heavy and can be thick with hay dust. And, always, there are the flies. In hauling hay or livestock, there are those flies, and they get into everything. They are inside the air-conditioned cab, your sandwich, your face . . . you name it and they are there. Flies seem to be bigger and more aggressive when you are loading in the summer at Imperial Valley . . . when the mercury soars into the triple digits.

Cool, dry weather aside, there are some good tools that make a world of difference in loading (and unloading) hay and alfalfa. A good set of hay hooks for placing the smaller bales is a definite requirement, a leather apron or chaps (like the cowboys wear) would also be necessary, and a good, strong back is absolutely essential. It probably wouldn't hurt to keep the name and phone number of a good chiropractor handy, either. Just how much weight can be hauled largely depends on what kind of combination the truck or trailers are.

77

Buz Shoemaker's long-hood Kenworth is pictured here off-loading a cargo of hay-squeeze cubes. A 425-horsepower Detroit Diesel gets this rig down the road.

Waldo Owens of Alhambra, California, put over a million miles on this 1940s "L" Model Mack. Colors were dark green and white.

Johnson Bros. of Ellensburg, Washington, can haul heavier loads because more axles can carry more weight. The pull-trailer has four axles for greater payload.

Generally, 26 tons would be a normal load. However, try pulling this amount, going up Whitewater Grade with headwinds that almost stop you in your tracks! Add a 110-degree temperature and a radiator that is telling you that its time to replace it, and you have the ingredients for turning your trip into a "true adventure."

Most of the hay haulers from the Chino area of California get their loads from the Imperial Valley area. However, it is not uncommon to see trucks bringing in loads from Nevada and Utah. Northern hay will usually remain within that geographic area, and the same holds true for hay in other parts of the country, too, because it may be too difficult or too expensive to transport hay long distances before it rots or molds. There are exceptions, however, where hay or alfalfa may be hauled from Canada to as far away as Florida, when a specialty product is desired. But, in general, truckers who transport hay are home more often than their counterparts in produce hauling, who may run coast-to-coast. Interestingly, though hay haulers tend to run relatively close to home, many hay trucks have sleeper cabs.

Given the tiring, hot labor involved in hauling hay, hay truckers prefer to work in the cooler hours of the day, especially during the summer. It may be better to load at 10:00 p.m. than at 10:00 a.m., and for this reason, one can see hay trucks running down the highways at all hours of the day — and night.

What concerns most of the truckers who haul hay is how fast they can load their truck, how fast they can unload their truck, and how fast they can get their paycheck. Needless to say, the more loads that can be hauled, the more money that can be made.

Securing loads can be "fun," as the law is quite clear on how hay and alfalfa are to be tied down. Any deviation from established practice can and does result in heavy fines imposed by local law enforcement or by the Highway Patrol. Standard equipment includes one-inch rope, a safety chain, a "come-along" (to cinch the load together), and V-boards for front and back portions of the load. And, of course, DOT permits and insurance are a must if a trucker is going to be legal in this profession.

Here, we see a White-Freightliner pulling for El Monte Hay Market. The older pull trailers had three axles.

Tarping the load is not necessary as a rule, and early-cut hay can take a lot more punishment than a load of dry summer hay. Though this can sometimes vary depending on expected weather during transit, or even the animals to which the hay will be fed, because some animals are less tolerant of wet or moldy hay.

Oddly, wet, moldy hay and alfalfa can actually become a combustible fire hazard if tightly packed in some barns. Also, any spark that lands on a dry bale of hay, and fanned by the wind can cause a fire that is difficult to put out. Likewise, if truck exhaust stacks are too close to the hay, the heat could ignite a fire, which is why some older, conventional trucks of the 1940s and 1950s had their exhaust stacks exit either through the center of the hood or out the side of the hood.

As hay hauling becomes easier, thanks to advancements in transportation technology, it is not too surprising to see companies like J. B. Hunt hauling Hay Squeeze bales. However, for those truckers carrying 426 smaller bales weighing 125 pounds each, there is no substitute for experience and skill.

This 1952 GMC was owned and used by Phil Troost before he sold it and moved his dairy to New Mexico from California.

In this 1971 picture, we see Dick Cano's Peterbilt cab-over in San Fernando, California. This rig was painted by George Barris, the famous custom car designer and painter. Power is supplied by an 8V71 Detroit Diesel.

Bull Rohr runs this 1952 Peterbilt cab-over from his farm in Creston, California. Hay and alfalfa haulers used this kind of equipment in the 1950s.

ogy finally gave trucking a true, appreciable edge over the horse teams.

Until the 1940s and early 1950s, many of the log trucks were underpowered, relying upon gasoline engines to produce power. Trucks and tractors like the Ford F-8 models, the KB-8 and KB-11 models from International, plus the High-Torque Chevrolet and GMC trucks were popular trucks with the lumber industry. Also common were various military trucks, once used in World War II, which found new uses in the forests, moving logs instead of weapons, troops or military supplies. And, not to be forgotten, were the Diamond Ts and Whites of the era. For most log haulers, the larger Kenworths, Peterbilts, Autocars, and Sterlings existed only on their "wish lists," because their prices were just too high.

Roads were another thing that improved, literally paving the way for more trucks to move into the woods. Forty years ago, major roads were few and far between, which made the task of log hauling both treacherous and dangerous. County roads were unpaved, which made matters worse. And forestry roads just weren't meant for log trucks;

A load of logs from Bryce Canyon, Utah, is seen being unloaded at the mill in Fredonia, Arizona. Reidhead Lumber in Fredonia owns this Kenworth, as well as several others in its log-hauling operations

they weren't wide enough to handle a tractor/trailer combination, and when it rained they became muddy bogs that challenged the best of log haulers and their underpowered trucks.

When it wasn't raining, such as during the long, hot summer months, logging roads became dusty making it not only impossible for a trucker to keep a rig clean, but it also severely hampered visibility — especially if forced to follow another truck into or out of the woods. Many times, an existing road was improved upon with one "swipe" of a Cat or bulldozer, but the improvements lasted only until the first rain, and in some cases, the "improvement" actually made the roads worse, by uncovering large rocks, or tree roots that served as major obstacles for truckers.

Some of the logging roads remain a challenge today to all but four-wheel drive vehicles. And log haulers can't afford to be wimps or feel intimidated by driving near the edge of a high cliff. It's all part of a day work's for a log hauler.

Tires have improved greatly through the years. In earlier times, the tires on the log trucks and trailers were the bias-ply type, which meant that if the tractor or trailer tire hit a large rock or tree stump the tire would go flat. Flat tires, while an inconve-

nience to any trucker, were especially a problem to the log hauler of the 1940s and 1950s, as there were no cellular phones, and most of the owner/operators can't afford either road mechanics or tire repairmen. Needless to say, changing a tire was no "walk in the park" for the unlucky trucker faced with this problem. Especially in soft, muddy, or uneven ground.

Lighting, too, has received considerable attention. On early logging trucks, lighting was somewhat of a luxury, since clearance and tail lights would usually only last for one trip. Fortunately, in those early days, the Highway Patrol and local police frequently allowed for such malfunctions and the laws were enforced more in spirit rather than by the letter. Today, Light-Emiting Diodes (LEDs) are both more durable, plus shine a brighter light than conventional lights, which makes trucking much safer for truckers, loggers, and the public.

Ask any veteran trucker what the greatest invention has been for trucking, though, and most will credit the engine brake, or "Jake" brake, so-named after the company that invented it in 1961, Jacobs Manufacturing. Their allegiance is well-founded, too, when you consider the fear and horror that must go through the mind of a log hauler going downhill with 76,000-pound gross vehicle weight, without anything to stop them except the lowest of gears in their underpowered "gas-jobs."

Another top pick invention-wise would have to be one of trucking's most infamous: the CB radio. Prior to the popularity of the citizens band (CB) radio, truck drivers used hand signals to communicate with each other, mainly to warn of trouble ahead — cops, traffic accidents, weigh stations, or police check points — thus giving oncoming drivers a chance to take appropriate action. And if a trucker was en route back into the woods, and he met empty log trucks coming out of the woods, he knew that was a sign that a logger had been killed nearby, and the truckers were returning empty as a somber sign of respect.

Sadly, one of the most common ways that loggers were killed in the past was by loading logs onto the trucks and trailers. It was dangerous, dirty work that commonly required brute force that put men directly in harm's way, either between two

huge, heavy logs, or between the logs and truck or trailer. In fact, the work was so dangerous that more loggers were killed and injured in loading logs than in any other phase of logging.

With today's technology and the sophistication of the machinery, however, loading and unloading logs is much safer, plus can be performed at a faster pace. Still, there is always an element of danger when people are working near large, moving equipment and heavy cargo.

Some of that equipment, though, has actually been getting lighter in recent years, while at the same time getting larger, too. Today's trailers are made of stronger, lighter-weight materials that allow them to be larger and carry bigger payloads . . . and that means higher profits.

On average, about 4,000 board-feet can be transported on a log truck. A load of smaller logs will be about 3,500 board-feet, with big logs bringing about 5,500 board-feet. And while many mo-

A Western Star is seen here in British Columbia. Canadian-built, the Western Star is quite popular with truckers whose profession is log hauling.

Seen here at an antique truck show is a Kenworth with its load of logs. Settlemier Trucking of Castle Rock, Washington, is the owner of this tractor/trailer combo.

torists may think a log is a log is a log, there are many different kinds of wood that get trucked down the highways. For example, in Washington and Oregon, fir, cedar and pine are most commonly cut, while harvesting in California may also include redwood and some oak. And other states will have trees common to their regions.

The trucks — which are usually either part of a truck and trailer or tractor/trailer combination, or, in Idaho and parts of Montana, pulling two or more trailers — have received their share of improvements, too. Now they have more horsepower, power steering, air conditioning, and all the other amenities that others in trucking enjoy. And gone are the days of three-stick shifting, while Jake brakes can be found on just about all of the logging trucks. Contemporary trucks and trailers have bunks and stakes to hold the logs in place, instead of the older "cheese blocks," used in holding the outside logs in place.

Getting those logs loaded is a fairly quick process today, but getting them unloaded is quite a bit quicker — with today's equipment, unloading may take only a few minutes. And when the logs are loaded, they're done more safely by resting on bunks, while stakes, chains, and binders secure the load for its trip from the forest to a nearby mill.

After the logs are unloaded, each mill or log yard has a trailer loader that lifts a trailer up and places it on a truck, because the roads are often narrow and not paved, preventing the trucks from jostling around to get properly positioned.

Because logging loads are generally only run from the woods to a mill that's usually only a few miles away, log haulers are generally able to be home every night. But that doesn't necessarily make it an easy life; a typical day may see a log hauler starting at 3:00 in the morning and making two or three trips from the woods to the mill and

back. But to keep things fair between drivers, log haulers typically work in a rotating sequence, so today's lead driver — who might get three runs in, while the rest of the driver's each can only do two — will be at the end of the driving line tomorrow, where he may only make one or two runs. Eventually, everyone rotates through the lead, this way every trucker gets his fair share of the hauling.

As is the case in all phases of trucking, the log hauler faces his share of problems. The main problem is the availability of logs, because the U.S. Forest Service has made logging "off limits" in many parts of the forests. To make the situation worse for the smaller operator, the mills and the larger logging companies seem to be getting most of the work . . . but even they can't always remain profitable enough to stay in business, begging the question of how can the little guy do it, if the big guys can't?

Even with all of its problems and a questionable future, driving a log truck still brings with it a certain sense of satisfaction that only those who haul logs know. Log haulers can savor the sounds of their powerful engines as they run through the mountains, forests, near lakes, and peacefully coexist with the local wildlife.

Ray Collins Logging in British Columbia owns this nice-looking B Model Mack. This is the way log trucks look, when they are running empty.

Chapter 9

Lumber Hauling

Building a Better Future

If you're building a picnic table, chances are pretty good that your average family car — or at least a mini pickup truck — can haul all the lumber you need for the project. But if you're building a house or an office building or some other sizable structure, you need lots of lumber — far too much for even a heavy-duty one-ton full-size pickup. That's when you need a professional lumber hauler, like those employed by most lumber yards. With a single trip, they can often haul all the lumber needed to frame up a house, whereas a contractor would have to make literally dozens of trips with his pickup truck — each of which would not only raise the price of the construction, but would add considerable delays to the work schedule.

As with most forms of trucking, hauling lumber has changed dramatically over the years, particularly in terms of the equipment used to handle the jobs. In early times, roll-trucks, that could unload without the use of a forklift, were a common sight. Also there was the use of bar-trucks, which consisted of a truck and trailer with steel bars tacked to both the truck body (across the frame), and pull trailer. These bar-trucks were popular, because they were a lot lighter than either roll-trucks or truck-and-trailer combos thanks to their wood bed. Loading and unloading bar trucks was also easier than with other types of trucks.

A Mack Superliner owned by Atlas Lumber is seen here at their facility. Truck and trailer configurations are a popular combination for lumber haulers in the West.

In this 1956 picture, we seen Don Stanfield's 1950 Kenworth leased to Chuck Keesey. Colors of this rig were dark blue and white. Truckers Paradise was a favorite "watering hole" for lumber haulers in the Los Angeles area in the 1950s.

Just as all lumber-hauling trucks aren't created equal, neither are the loads they haul. Unlike steel or heavy machinery, which can be easily and safely secured by chains, bundles of wood must be attached with straps, to prevent damaging the wood. Some loads of lumber may require a strap over the bottom units or bundles, as well as three more straps over the top bundles, depending upon both the size and length of the load — the longer the load, the more straps a trucker needs to safely secure the load during transit.

Before the use of straps, heavy cable was used to tie down the lumber. Corner irons were used under the cable on good lumber so that the cable would not cut into, or damage, the cargo. A winch bar or cheater pipe is used for leverage to tighten down the straps or cables so that the load is tightly secured. These straps go on a slot on a winch with a ratchet that holds the strap or cable tight.

Because lumber can be easily damaged by moisture, exhaust smoke, and other contaminants, use of tarps is necessary. Tarps may also be used in hot, dry climates like those of Utah and Arizona. This is done to protect the lumber from the hot, dry desert winds that can cause the front of the boards to crack. Tarps are frequently used when a lumber truck is loaded or operated in mountain areas where cinder rock is used on the roadway to melt the snow. If this cinder is allowed to collect on the edges of the lumber, this will result in the dulling of saw blades, when the lumber is cut or processed at the plant.

It's easy to understand why it's so important for lumber haulers to know how to properly secure and protect their cargo. Equally important, of course, is knowing how to drive in dangerous mountain areas, because a sharp turn taken too fast can result in the loss of the load . . . or worse!

Beyond knowing how to drive in the mountains and what personal limits and those of the equipment are, a lumber hauler must know how to properly load the truck — where to place the bundles of lumber on both the truck and trailer, in order to keep axle weights evenly and legally distributed.

Sometimes, certain loads required additional measures to remain legal, such as when a load extended beyond the body or trailer — a situation that requires red lights to be attached to the over-hung portion to draw the attention of motorists and pedestrians, for safety reasons. During daylight driving, red flags are often used in place of the red lights, which could be tough to see in bright light. Most states have laws requiring loads that extend more than four feet beyond the truck or trailer to sport the red lights or flags.

Generally such oversize loads are only a local — or at best, a regional — problem, since most lumber shipped cross-country travels by rail. Of course, not

Seen here being loaded is a late-model Peterbilt operated by Hagle Lumber of Somis, California. Hauling lumber brings with it certain joys and problems not experienced by others in trucking.

This fleet picture shows the Peterbilts that are used to haul for Terry Lumber and its many retail stores.

all lumber goes by train for those long-distance trips; many large companies have numerous trucks intended for just such jobs. And, like freight haulers and many other truckers, long-distance lumber haulers will generally try to return hauling just about anything to further offset costs . . . and maybe even make a little profit. Sadly, independent truckers have a hard time getting a back-haul; in many cases, all they'll end up hauling home is their own pull trailer atop their truck body, assuming, of course, that they're driving a truck and trailer combination.

Even worse than the problem of not being able to find back-haul jobs is the fact that more and more lumber mills are closing, which is making it more and more difficult to obtain loads at all. And then there's the problem of the weather: The mills that are tucked away in the hills and mountains can be quite hazardous to reach, confronting a lumber hauler with rain, ice, snow, and fog, or some combinations of these.

Overall, however, hauling lumber, like hauling logs, takes the trucker into some of the most beautiful country in the world — much of which is seldom, if ever, seen by more than a handful of people.

This 1965 picture shows a rare truck, made by Brown Truck Co. The rig was used to haul lumber for Woolfolk Bros. Lumber of Buckner, Virginia.

In this 1967 picture, an International Emeryville is seen here as a truck and trailer loaded with lumber

Chapter 10

The Bedbug Haulers
Moving Families Together

There is an old saying that says, "You never get a second chance to make a first impression," and nowhere is this more true than with those truckers driving for the various van lines, or moving and storage outfits, known in the trucking industry as "The Bedbug Haulers." Moving people's personal possessions requires the trucker to be a public relations representative for his or her van line, in addition to a grunt laborer. This is very important if the client is a large corporate giant, where the trucker is often judged by his or her personality, personal appearance, and how their equipment (tractor and trailer) looks.

While others in trucking deliver to warehouses, feedlots, farms, factories, and refineries, those in the profession of hauling furniture, computers, or trade show exhibits often have direct contact with the public. While there are truckers that may look like ZZ Top band members, most of the van lines prefer their operators to look more like Clark Kent (of Superman fame) — neat, clean, and presentable.

Hauling furniture and personal possessions differs completely from other types of trucking. For one thing, each noncartoned item must be wrapped in special furniture pads to protect it

Founded in 1891, Bekins Van Lines is a household name in the moving industry. Seen here at a truck show is Dan Campbell's sharp-looking Kenworth cab-over. This truck was last seen painted Mayflower Van Lines colors and pulling for a Mayflower agent in New England. Many of the truckers who lease to the van lines often change companies until they find the one that suits them best.

Donnie Cornelison leased this International, circa 1987, to North American Van Lines of Ft. Wayne, Indiana. Many of the owner/operators with the various van lines take pride in their rigs, as can be seen in this truck.

during the move. And second, it takes longer to both load and unload, because each item has to be inventoried, and notes must be made regarding whatever items may be damaged prior to transporting. Detailed inventory records greatly reduce the number of claims that might arise from a cross-country trip.

Generally, one shipment a day is loaded into a 53-foot trailer; however, loads weighing 5,000 pounds or less can be loaded in multiple shipments. At this rate, it is normal to take a week or more to completely fill up the trailer. Of course, a lot depends upon the size of the shipment as well as the loading and delivery times.

Van lines realized long ago that the moving process is a very traumatic one for the family or business on the move, so the trucker's job changed from one of just driver and loader, to diplomat and customer service representative. Furthermore, good

Bedbug rigs come in many shapes and sizes. The Peterbilt seen here is leased to an Allied Van Lines agent in Minnesota. The tractor has a regular sleeper behind the cab, and a "Penthouse" bunk, located above the driver. The drom box, behind the cab, allows for additional payload space.

organizational skills are needed in the loading and unloading, to not only ensure the truck is loaded, but that the mountains of paperwork gets filled out completely, and finally for hiring additional people to load and unload cargo. Of course, a really good furniture mover generally does his or her own loading, giving it that personal touch, applying years of experience to hopefully ensure everything arrives at its destination in the exact same condition in which it left its original home.

Because everything has to be loaded by hand, loading a 53-foot furniture van takes a lot longer than the loading of a 53-foot freight trailer. In general, an experienced furniture hauler, with the aid of one helper, can load 1,000 pounds an hour and another 500 pounds with the aid of a third helper. However, like all other types of trucking, there are the variables that come into play. For instance, lugging a piano up ten flights of stairs or

Founded in 1928, Pyramid Van Lines had maroon for its earlier colors, then changed to white with green and blue trim. They were based out of South San Francisco, California. This picture, taken in Tucson in 1967, shows a White-Freightliner with a drom box and 40-foot trailer.

waiting for an elevator that runs in slow motion will exact some sort of delay. Toss in the occasional winter blizzard and you have the makings of a classic Laurel and Hardy comedy.

On average, a 53-foot, drop-frame furniture trailer will have upward of 4,600 cubic feet of load space. At an average of seven pounds per cubic feet, a good loader should be able to load around 32,000 to 33,000 pounds. That equates to about five families' belongings, at an average of about 6,500 pounds per family. Naturally, though, the weight of an "average" family's belongings often can and does vary, but with a maximum gross weight of about 80,000 pounds for a fully loaded 53-foot drop-frame trailer plus its cargo, there is usually plenty of room for a full load of several families' belongings.

Just like some loads are hard, some bedbug haulers get lucky and occasionally get an easy load. Easy loads are ones that have a lot of boxed items, which usually have good weight density to them and are easily stacked in the trailer. Add good access at both loading and unloading points, and you have the ideal haul. But, this is the exception and not generally the rule. There is a flip-side, and this can and often does include the hauling of brittle and antique furniture, all too common to HHG (household goods) movers. Antique furniture generally has longer and more numerous legs than contemporary furniture, which means that loads are more bulky and take up a lot of space in the

This sharp-looking 1968 White-Freightliner was owned by Bob Luedeke of Claremont, California. Freightliner had an assembly factory in Pomona (close to Claremont), and Luedeke was at the plant every day, seeing his truck as it was being built. Like the rigs owned by United Parcel Service (UPS), Luedeke did not believe in displaying the logo or insignia of the truck maker on his tractor. An 8V71 Detroit Diesel supplied the power for this rig.

trailer. That kind of situation makes for poor density, and truckers have to be more careful to make sure that any previous damage is noted and recorded on the invoice, otherwise claims for damaged furniture can be charged against the trucker. When claims for damaged furniture do arise, the larger van lines have their own department that can resolve the matter. This is also true if something is lost in transit. Generally speaking, if the trucker either breaks or loses it, he or she will pay for it. For

Here we see an early 1960s International Emeryville pulling for Engel Bros. of Elizabeth, New Jersey. The International Emeryville, built from the mid-1950s until 1965, was a favorite among many of the bedbug haulers.

this reason, it is absolutely essential that the operator doing the hauling make a detailed inventory of what is on board, and its exact condition prior to closing the back of the trailer doors.

And once the trailer's loaded and those doors are closed, the driver still has to haul it. Rural and suburban stops are frequently easy deliveries (and pick-ups), since traffic is generally light, and there are generally plenty of areas to turn around in and to park. But not all stops go so smoothly; pulling a 53-foot trailer into Boston or Brooklyn can truly test a trucker's skill, patience, and guts. Cruising into a high-crime neighborhood with a tractor-trailer rig is a quick way to become a moving target. And when a driver isn't worrying about thugs and gangs, he has to be wary of the cops; delivering a single office chair up 43 flights into the Arco Towers in downtown Los Angeles will give a ticket-hungry meter maid plenty of time to cite your tractor, plus time leftover to write out an additional ticket for the trailer, all in the name of maintaining quotas. No, the bedbug hauler's life isn't really an easy one. In fact, many truckers would argue it's one of the hardest careers you could pick: it has long hours of hard manual loading, long hauls that keep them away from home, unknown hazards at pick-up and drop-off points, plus they have to put on a happy face and deal with the public a lot. All of which can be quite trying.

As with the rest of the trucking industry, governmental deregulation increased competition, which lowered rates for hauling HHG. The moving industry has been particularly devastated by the deregulation. Because it's now fairly easy to get into the moving industry, thus lots of new "players" have entered the market with poorly trained, poorly paid employees plus poorly maintained equipment. Usually, these "fly-by-night" companies are "here today and gone tomorrow." In the interim, they have hurt the longtime reliable companies by cutting rates on long-distance moves. Even worse, the poor service offered by these flash-in-the-pan movers has given a "black eye" to the HHG industry as a whole.

Over the past 20 years, there has been a slow, but steady decline in the number of larger, established carriers. As is often the case, no one specific problem is to blame. Some of the decline can be traced to military and defense cutbacks, which cut back the number of military personnel, and thus the van lines' main market — moving military families from base to base following reassignments. Higher labor costs, lower rates, and poor management have all factored in, as well.

Zane Bradshaw leased this "Crackerbox" GMC to Greyhound Van Lines, based in Chicago. In the 1970s, Smythe Van Lines took over Greyhound, and trade show exhibits became their specialty. They were also popular in Hawaii with moving military families.

Many of the largest van lines are located in Indiana. Red Ball Van Lines of Indianapolis is one of these companies. A GMC is seen here, parked behind Shorty Campbell's Truck Stop in Rosemead, California.

"When You Move, Neptune Cares," was the motto of Neptune Van Lines, a pioneer mover of computers. This photo depicts a 5000 series White that was one of the many leased to the New Rochelle, New York-based company. Colors were cream with red trim.

Currently, the Department of Transportation oversees a lot of what the van lines do and how they conduct their business, but there is talk that the Department of Consumer Affairs may eventually have more control and authority over this phase of trucking. There are pros and cons to both sides of such an arrangement, and only time will tell what will happen.

To survive, many van lines have expanded divisions of their business that were formerly only sidelines. For example, many of the larger van lines have their domestic furniture hauling, plus a division devoted to handling trade show business, which formerly accounted for only a small portion of a van line's business. While hauling furniture is basically a door-to-door operation, the trade show truckers haul most of their contents in crated forms, running coast-to-coast to convention centers in larger cities, and often on a tight schedule.

To stay competitive and provide good value, many van lines have taken advantage of new technologies that have eased coast-to-coast moves considerably. Gone are the days when a single-axle, gas-burning tractor pulled a 32-foot round-nose single-axle dropdeck trailer. Instead, we now regularly see 53-foot trailers, some tandems, and often spread-axles that ride on tubeless tires and air-ride suspension. Contemporary tractors are powered by 400-horsepower diesel engines, with twin-screw rear ends and, in many cases, sport huge, self-contained sleepers that have all the comforts of home for a trucker — including the kitchen sink.

Giving bedbug haulers everything they need to do a good job carries over to the trailer, too. Today's bedbug trailers usually include at least 18 dozen furniture pads, 12 dozen skins, three two-

wheel dollies, eight four-wheel dollies (for moving items like stoves, washers, and other heavy items), 300 "rubber bands" or bungee cords, 28 aluminum decking boards, 12 sheets of 4x8-foot plywood, 24 logistic straps, eight car tie-downs, one set of split ramps (for loading automobiles inside the trailer), and miscellaneous equipment for building tailgates for overloads on the back of the trailer. Like the boy scouts, or perhaps more appropriately, the Marines, movers pride themselves on being prepared for anything.

So far, hauling HHG may have sounded like a job for which only the masochistic need apply, but it does have its advantages over other segments of the trucking industry. Chief among those advantages — in spite of deregulation — is pay. Quite simply, loading and unloading all that furniture is a lot of physical work, and the movers get paid well for their time and effort. And contrary to common belief, movers also enjoy more free time at home, though rarely in the summer, which is typically the mover's busy season, when families are more likely to relocate.

Unfortunately, summer time isn't the ideal time to move, in a trucker's eyes. Instead, the best time of year to haul for a van line is when the temperature hovers around 70 degrees. In the sweltering heat of the summer, the inside of a 53-foot van can become an oven, making physical work quite unbearable.

Whenever moving vans do roll out, the van lines will always try to make the most of a run by getting truckers back-loads for their trip back home to their families. This isn't always possible, because of the many variables in trucking, but a progressive large carrier will try to make every effort to do so. After all, more loads mean more profit.

Many people in the industry believe that the future of the bedbug industry may involve two distinct operations, along the same lines as the current HHG and trade show divisions. The first type of operations would be service-driven, focusing on large corporate accounts for not just trade shows, but actual moves, as well. The second type would be the HHG carrier, which would focus on the C.O.D. customer who needs to relocate. These HHG carriers would be more generic in nature than the corporate carriers, and would have to compete at least indirectly with the likes of U-Haul and Ryder truck rental companies for customers moving dollars.

But even now, not all van lines are created equal, and the differences between them can be very substantial.

Carl Steinbrick leased this 1960 White-Freightliner to Republic Van Lines, once based in Los Angeles. The logo of two ducks in flight with the words, "Easy Moving," was a familiar sign as the Republic trucks crossed the nation.

A 1968 Peterbilt with an 8V71 Detroit Diesel engine is seen here pulling for Lyon Van Lines, based in Los Angeles. In earlier days, the Lyon rigs were painted all silver.

Interestingly enough, there is only about an eight percentage point-spread in terms of pay between carriers and owner/operators. The real differences start to appear in the customer base. Today's trend is for an owner/operator to lease out to a large booking agent that has a lot of influence with the parent van line, which helps keep the trucker busy with the main van line, in case the booker doesn't have the tonnage necessary to keep his lessors busy with the booking agent's business. In other words, the large multimillion dollar booker has more clout with the "home office" in getting a load for one of its truckers, than if the trucker tried to get a load on his or her own. Also, larger booking agents have their own claims departments, which makes claims easier on the trucker, if and when they arise.

Some agents are always looking for new owner/operators, usually because of quick turnover related to either poor business or slow payment of the owner/operators they had formerly contracted. On the other hand, there are booking agents that have a waiting list of truckers, a reputation for prompt payment, fair treatment, and steady work. So, for many owner/operators, it pays to carefully check out the reputation of booking agents before signing any contracts.

Of particular interest should be the level and quality of communication between the van line and the owner/operator, because it is the most important ingredient for a successful partnership. This can be a complicated issue at times, too, since many people are involved in the shipment of household goods. Ultimately, though, each carrier generally has at least one person where "the buck stops." In other words, there should always be a fair

and impartial person in a management position within the van lines who is capable of rendering decisions based upon common sense and fairness to all parties concerned. This may not be an easy thing to do, but if there is to be good communication at all levels, the van lines need this kind of liaison.

Understandably, pay is a primary concern for any trucker. Most of the major van lines pay their truckers every two weeks, though there are a few outfits that settle with their leased operators once a month, and still others that will pay within 48 hours of receiving all necessary paperwork from the trucker.

Even though most truckers prefer to load a load themselves, there are times when that simply isn't practical, times when they need help. If a trucker should decide he needs or wants help, the extra hands are paid for out of his own pocket, not by the larger carrier to whom the trucker is contracted. Most truckers choose to pay workers by the hour, but in parts of the South, workers are paid by the amount of weight that is loaded or unloaded. As a result, many truckers will seek the services of the local unemployment department or some form of manpower service.

The life of a bedbug operator is unlike that of any other kind of trucker, so anyone contemplating a career in the moving industry is advised to ride with a trucker who is leased to some larger carrier to see firsthand whether that's the life that you truly want. Being a bedbug hauler can be very rewarding, both monetarily and in terms of job satisfaction, but it can also be back- and knee-breaking work that can leave you in agonizing pain at the end of the day.

Chapter 11

Rolling Billboards

Taking the Message on the Road

Any business, no matter what it sells or does, needs customers. To get customers, a business has to make sure customers know it exists, and that generally means it has to advertise. And for many companies, outfitting their trucks and trailers with attractive, effective advertising messages is just good, cost-effective business.

Think of the trucks you frequently see on the highway. While many may feature blank walls, many sport the logos of the companies for which they haul, including McDonald's, Coca-Cola, various beer companies, grocery stores, and others. Many of these companies aren't in the business of trucking to turn a profit; they're in it out of necessity — it's the cheapest method through which they can deliver products to stores or even consumers directly. But good business sense dictates that companies maximize the value they get from every dollar they spend, and one way they do that with trucks and trailers is to give them two duties: first, to haul product; second, to promote it. And when you think of it, the mix is a natural pairing. After all, what better way could there be for getting the public's attention than to roll a billboard by them on a long, boring highway, when their mind is readily open to stimulation?

Graphic markings can range from the sublime to those that "jump out" at you. Sony Sound Systems decided to go the "full nine yards," and match their trailer to their Ford tractor. A tractor/trailer, with graphics like this, makes millions of impressions with the motoring public as it runs coast-to-coast.

Rogelio Velasquez drove this Kenmex (Mexican Kenworth) from Colima, Mexico, to Los Angeles with its trailer full of mangos. In Mexico, truckers know the power of graphics, as can be seen on this trailer.

Brewing companies have always known the value of putting graphics on their trucks and trailers in order to promote their products. In this 1965 picture, taken near Toledo, Ohio, we see an Autocar with its trailer neatly matched, marketing Stroh's Beer.

Even companies that don't have consumer-oriented products or services are getting into the rolling billboards business by selling advertising space on the sides of their trailer fleets to companies that are anxious to make the most of this developing new advertising medium. And the ad dollars are helping to bolster income for many companies that have been hard hit in these deregulated times.

And while some businesses may complain that advertising costs money, most know that the old adage "You have to spend money to make money" still holds true. And to these companies, turning trucks into rolling billboards is a proven method of getting valuable exposure. And there are independent studies that back up their beliefs.

"Let's Have a Party" was an International from the 1950s. It is seen here taking out a load for Hawaiian Punch.

To most truckers that run up and down Interstate 15, the name of Hardwick & Hand is synonymous with powder-train (bulk cement) rigs, but at one time Hardwick & Hand meant the finest in meats and smaller markets in the Victorville, California, area. The graphics on this 1961 "Crackerbox" GMC were in style for 1966 when this picture was taken.

In this 1970 picture, we see one of Bert Rapp's Peterbilts that he ran cross-country for Ingersoll-Rand. Big, bold graphics get the message across.

In a study conducted by a San Francisco, California, advertising agency, the costs of rolling billboards (tractor/trailers) were compared to those of television commercials — and the trucks came out on top, by a wide margin. Comparing prices, the expense of dressing up a trailer using fleet graphics, broke down to a cost of 22 cents for every thousand people who viewed the trailer — less than one-tenth that of traditional television advertising, which priced out at $2.90 per thousand viewers. Adding to the value is the fact that the life span of a decorated trailer can be anywhere from one year to a lifetime, depending on the particular message applied. Even if a trailer had been outfitted with graphics and logos to last only seven years, the same ad agency study calculated that the money spent on the trailer would yield a 7:1 return on the initial cost of detailing the trailer.

Put another way, the average stationary billboard makes 300,000 impressions each year — that's the number of times motorists and passengers see this billboard (not necessarily how many people see it, though, since some people may see the billboard over and over). On the other hand, rolling billboards can make better than 10 million impressions, and a much as 16 million impressions if the semis are running coast-to-coast. And since large stationary billboards can cost from $1,500 to

In this picture, we see a Kenworth cab-over truck and trailer, circa 1958, pulling for Bardahl, a famous automotive additive. Actually, this rig was operating for D&O Transport of Yakima, Washington, and was loaded with apples. Coloring of this rig was white, with green and black graphics

Ol' Blue® USA takes the message of highway safety to both the truckers and school kids, thanks to its loyal sponsors, law enforcement, and this 53-foot trailer. This rig can be seen at truck shows coast-to-coast

$4,000 or more per month to rent, it's easy to see how a one-time decorating cost for a 48-foot trailer can really be a bargain.

How much it costs to decorate a trailer is somewhat dependent upon the actual method used to apply graphics to the trailer, and there are basically two options from which to choose. One method is to use marking materials that are available from a variety of companies including Avery and 3M. Given who makes them, it's not too surprising that this method of trailer decoration relies on affixing large, pressure-sensitive decals to the trailers. Decals can have many advantages, not the least of which are cost, ease, and speed of application, ease of customization, plus a variety of finishes, colors, and effects, such as reflective materials that "light-up" when vehicle headlights hit them.

The other side of the coin is the old standby: Paint. Here, the belief is that the paint will hold up to the abuse of foul weather and repeated washings better than the decals, however, this hasn't been

proven entirely true. And given the many advantages of decals, painted-on graphics are quickly becoming a thing of the past.

Conversely, the wave of the future may just be 3M's Scotchprint System, which has simplified the creation of large and complex fleet graphics by allowing an image — a picture of a product, some words, or a company or product logo, for example — to be scanned into a computer, recorded digitally, then cropped and sized as needed. Colors can be changed and different text can be merged to customize messages for specific markets, products, or promotions. The completed design is then printed and transferred to film that can be applied to the truck or trailer. Actual application by an experienced pro takes approximately eight hours for a 48-foot trailer.

A nice bonus feature of decals is that they can be removed without leaving a gummy residue on the trailer, even without the use of any special chemical strippers or tools.

Little Irvy was a 38-foot, 20-ton whale that was kept frozen in this trailer. For several years, Little Irvy toured the country in this 1965 Kenworth owned by Jerry Malone. The graphics for this unit get right to the point.

With so much design flexibility, it's easy for companies to get carried away in creating graphics for their fleet. But good design principles dictate that getting the best "bang for the buck" means keeping the basic design both big and simple, because people will see your sign for only a short time as it drives by, and a cluttered image will prevent them from quickly getting your message.

For all the advantages of rolling billboards, they're still not a "free lunch"; there are disadvantages, too, namely negative publicity.

Negative publicity for a product or service can result when a tractor/trailer with graphics is driven in a reckless manner. Motorists tend to remember the bad even better than the good, and everyone knows how the news media capitalizes on negative experiences. And even if motorists didn't witness a trucker driving irresponsibly, seeing one pulled over on the side of the road by a cop implies that the driver was doing something he shouldn't have. And that big graphic on the side of that trailer is going to stick in their minds. And what of trucks involved in traffic accidents? Even if the accident wasn't the truckers fault, many motorists will often assume it was, and that big billboard of a trailer will give them a target for their mistaken anger.

There's yet another point worth pondering: The billboards advertise to any would-be thieves what they could expect to find inside the truck, were they to break into it. Now, that may not be a problem for a McDonald's reefer truck hauling a load of petrified burger patties and frozen fries, but a giant Sony on the side is as good as an "X" marking the spot of a treasure of CD players, camcorders, stereo receivers, and wide-screen televisions.

By and large, however, the advantages of having billboard-like graphics far outweigh the disadvantages. Plus good-looking tractors and trailers, with clear markings, words, and logos tend to enhance the public's perception of what trucking is all about. Furthermore, more conspicuous vehicles can add to the margin of safety, especially at night when reflective materials are used in the graphics. Other positive items include better driver morale, better customer reception, lower maintenance costs, and higher resale values — all of which can be traced to tasteful graphics.

Bob Reisner hauled special-built cars to various shows with this International-CO4000. The graphics for both tractor and trailer were completely handpainted, and the fade from yellow to red was wet-blended with several spray-painting applications. Lichtenberger Sign Company, truck lettering specialists since 1925, did the graphics and artwork.

Chapter 12

Standing Tall
The Big Rigs That Stand Apart

You are what you drive! All too often we see a motorist or trucker who is driving a vehicle that is in dire need of body and fender repair. As a result, the driver, in many cases, drives more careless. On the other side of the coin, we see cars and big rigs that show pride in ownership and, as a result, are driven in a more responsible manner.

Most of us remember the movie *Duel*, where a faceless tanker driver, in a beat-up old 1950s Peterbilt, chased down Dennis Weaver and tried to run him off the road. And unfortunately, a good portion of the general public is under the impression that all truckers operate in such sadistic manners. And while there may be some justification for such beliefs, even anti-trucking crusaders admit that the unsafe truckers that give professional trucking a black eye are the minority.

Yet, every day, we see big rigs in the wrong lanes on the freeways and interstates, following too closely and turning on their high-beams in the day in order to intimidate a slower moving four-wheeler in front of them. And the cops are nowhere to be seen . . . until they pull over a well-behaving trucker because a clearance light is malfunctioning.

Not to be dismayed by the poor reputation are those men and women who stand tall above the

Kevin Reber of Santa Clara, Utah, fixed up this 1978 long-hood Kenworth, known as "Midnight Fantasy." A Cummins KTA 600-horsepower engine fits snugly under the massive hood, backed by "two sticks" for transmissions. "Midnight Fantasy" was sold to Joe Sanchez, a trucker from Grants, New Mexico, and is used daily to haul produce.

Lyall Wiebe (pronounced Weeb) of Manitoba, Canada, owns "The Untouchable," a 1954 Peterbilt with Duesenberg headlights. The vital statistics include a 3406 Caterpillar engine, an 18-speed transmission on a 310-inch wheelbase. Weight for this showhorse is around 24,500 pounds. This unit can be seen at many truck show and gathers large crowds wherever it goes

rest of the trucking pack, trying desperately to present a clean, respectable image of what trucking can be.

These truckers choose to lead by example and spend countless hours maintaining, cleaning, and customizing their trucks — even company-owned trucks — to demonstrate their pride in what they do. Their trucks may sport fancy paint jobs, unusual graphics or eye-catching markings, vast expanses of chrome, even an abundance of lights or a combination of the above.

True, beauty is in the eye of the beholder, and many onlookers may ridicule a decked-out truck as "overkill," but all can appreciate a clean, well-cared for rig over a rusted, dirty, dilapidated truck. And some will actually like the excess.

While their custom rigs may not win them any additional contracts with shippers, the good these truckers do for the industry is immeasurable. And to them, our hats are off.

When Mike Stroud decided to sell his company and move out of California, he kept his pride and joy: this "Large Car" features a Double Eagle sleeper. Double Eagle prides itself on building custom sleepers for those truckers who want the finest. The tractor is a long-hood Peterbilt.

Bill Cross of Phillips Ranch, California, owns this long-hood 1979 Kenworth. Usually found hauling seafood from California to Florida, this rig sports a 296-inch wheelbase and has a 3406 Cat and a 15-speed transmission.

Tom Berg of Littleton, Colorado, owns this neat-looking Peterbilt Model 379 long-hood. This candy-apple red rig is leased to First Choice Trucking of Denver. Berg hauls perishables in the West with this truck.

The Freightliner, pictured here, was leased to Prime, Inc., of Springfield, Missouri. Trucks like this show the public that not all big rigs are "killer trucks" as some in the news media would like to have the public believe.

From Canada comes this Freightliner conventional with matching trailer. Here we see that the graphics from the tractor blend into its trailer. This kind of artwork does not come cheap, but when you consider the exposure-factor that this tractor and trailer receive as it runs down the interstates, the price is well worth the initial cost. The units are based in Canada and run "the lower 48."

Chapter 13

Famous Trucker's Trucks
Rolling Legends Past and Present

Just as in the railroad industry, where K. C. Jones was a "brave engineer," the trucking industry had its share of legendary drivers . . . some still alive, but many who have long since departed. The trucks featured in this section comprise only a few of the more famous truckers that drove them.

Swede Nelson generally runs out of Iowa to the East; however, this picture was taken circa 1982 on a trip he made to Los Angeles. Swede leased to Little Audrey's, a long-established reefer company from Fremont, Nebraska. Little Audrey's became part of Donco Carriers.

118

Joe Mustang of South El Monte, California, has trucked into just about every state with his 1957 H-63 Mack, since taking delivery of it in 1959. With a wheelbase of 264-inches, this Bulldog has a 1693-PCTA Caterpillar engine that cranks out 525 horsepower at the flywheel. The transmission is a 10-speed Fuller. The trailer, made by Brown Mfg., was purchased new in 1964 and is a 40-footer. Mustang has hauled anything that will fit on his trailer and, like Johnny Cash, always wears black.

This picture was taken in 1965 in North Lima, Ohio. The Diamond T seen here belonged to B.C. Fry of Independence, Iowa. B.C. Fry was "The Trucker's Trucker." B.C. generally ran at night, at speeds in three digits. Sadly, B.C. died in 1987, but his legend lives on . . . ask any old timer.

Blackie Skaggs bought this 1954 Kenworth new, from the Dallas Kenworth dealer in Texas. The KW was purchased in January of 1954 for $18,375, and ran it coast-to-coast until his death in 1997. The original 200-horsepower Cummins engine gave way to a Cummins Big Cam that put out 525 horses with a 13-speed transmission. Blackie specialized in hauling strawberries..

George Appleyard, III, of Winston-Salem, North Carolina, was a trucker that was years ahead of his time. Seen here in his 1967 Kenworth, in front of the White House, George was on his way to the ICC building to protest for deregulation. This was in 1969 and deregulation came about in 1980.

Women in trucking are a common sight today, but there was a time in the 1940s and 1950s when women had to prove themselves and, as a result, were often tougher than their male counterparts. This 1965 photo, taken in Toledo, Ohio, shows the Kenworth that was owned and operated by Corrine White. Corrine and Clara Hicks (known as The Pink Lady) blazed a trail in the history of trucking that only a few know of. Running coast-to-coast, both Corrine and Clara hauled whatever they could. Some called these truckers "hot freight" haulers, while others referred to them as "wildcat" truckers. Whatever they were called, these kinds of truckers received little recognition but saved many a shipper caught in a bind.

When Arnold Guril came to the United States in 1950, he had less than a dollar in his pockets. Over the next 40 years, he managed to buy four Kenworths. Seen in this 1972 picture, was his last purchase from J.T. Jenkins in Vernon, California. It was an extended-hood Kenworth with a 12V71 Detroit Diesel, backed by a five-speed main and four-speed auxiliary transmissions. Pulling for John. C. Whittaker, Arnold ran from Nogales, Arizona, to Canada, hauling produce.

Kenneth Lynch of Salt Lake City, ran the backroads from Los Angeles to the East, hauling whatever could fit in these former Roscoe Wagner cattle/produce bodies. The colors of this Kenworth were maroon and white.

In this 1957 picture, Bob Johnson's dark blue Kenworth is hooked to a 35-foot trailer. These units ran cross-country for Hartz Mountain Products.

Norm Fritz purchased this LT Mack on November 7, 1955, from the Mack dealer in Albuquerque for the grand sum of $18,280 — new! This was quite a sizable amount for 1955. The rig came equipped with a Cummins NHRBS 300-horsepower engine and a set of five and three transmissions. Norm went under the name of Western Steamship Supply and hauled whatever could fit in his trailer. Don Smith ran this truck from Los Angeles to Chicago, where it was stolen. Unfortunately, it was never recovered.

Chapter 14

Parting Shots

Taken in Colorado, these Peterbilts ran from Denver to Albuquerque for American Gypsum. The host truck would back-haul the other two, thus reducing deadheading.

How do you stop a wild elephant from charging? Cut up his credit cards or park this 1987 Kenworth in front of it! Bill & Wags Towing of Ontario, California, runs this heavy-duty wrecker both locally and for long-distance work. This truck is only one in a fleet of good-looking heavy-duty wreckers

Seen here in Indio, California, this 1966 Peterbilt was one of the very first with the tilt-hood. The truck and trailer seen here hauled propane and ammonia for Don Peabody, a one-time trucker for Watson Bros., who became owner of California Ammonia Transport of Anaheim. This truck featured a 335-horse Cummins engine with a five-speed main and four-speed auxiliary transmissions.

Bottom
Older trucks, from another era, rest in this 1967 picture taken in Fresno, California. The big rigs of the 1930s to the 1950s, while they were heavy and underpowered, were built to withstand the elements of time. Can this be said of today's trucks?

*Entire books can be written on truckers who transport auto-
mobiles. More and more, we see fancy trucks with their
loads on them like this Peterbilt*

*Randy Jordan, of Rajor Leasing, ran this old Corbitt coast-
to-coast in the 1950s and 1960s. Colors of this tractor
were yellow and white.*

Index